THE DEAD WRESTLER ELEGIES

✿

CHAMPIONSHIP EDITION

THE DEAD WRESTLER ELEGIES

❀

CHAMPIONSHIP EDITION

❀

W. TODD KANEKO

NEW MICHIGAN PRESS
TUCSON, ARIZONA

NEW MICHIGAN PRESS

DEPT OF ENGLISH, P. O. BOX 210067

UNIVERSITY OF ARIZONA

TUCSON, AZ 85721-0067

<http://newmichiganpress.com>

Orders and queries to <nmp@thediagram.com>.

ISBN 978-1-934832-82-0. FIRST PRINTING.

Design by Ander Monson.

Poems and art by W. Todd Kaneko.

CONTENTS

7

KAYFABE / KAY-FAYB / NOUN

Etymology: Believed to stem from carny slang for "protecting the secrets of the business." May come from a version of Pig Latin for "fake" ("ake-fay") or the phrase "be fake."

1. The portrayal of competition and storylines associated with professional wrestling as being authentic and not scripted or staged.

2. The work by wrestling performers to get an audience to suspend disbelief in order to manufacture authenticity for feuds, angles and gimmicks surrounding a professional wrestling match.

3. The strict observance of in-ring personalities and rivalries by wrestling performers in public, even when not wrestling or on camera, in order to protect the illusion that contests and storylines in professional wrestling are real.

for Caitlin

and for Leo, Dash, and Wiley

✾

1

I'm not on my death bed much nor will I be. I am not a quitter. —Harley Race, eight-time NWA World Heavyweight Champion

He started it all, the Strangler
choking men out with that yoke
of wrist and elbow. My father said
Ed Lewis was the greatest wrestler
of all time, that I was too young
to understand what that meant.
Don't trust a woman, he said,
until you know how it feels to lose
your breath. His mouth drooped
open, words flitting into dark
before I could identify those
shapes of their wings.

On television, the Macho Man
posed with his enormous cowboy hat
and Doink the Clown sprayed him
down with seltzer. It's a circus,
he said. No one appreciates men
like the Strangler anymore.
Outside, I imagined the world waiting
for my father to wrap it in his arms,
break it in three parts—one for me,
one for him and a knife curved
like my mother.

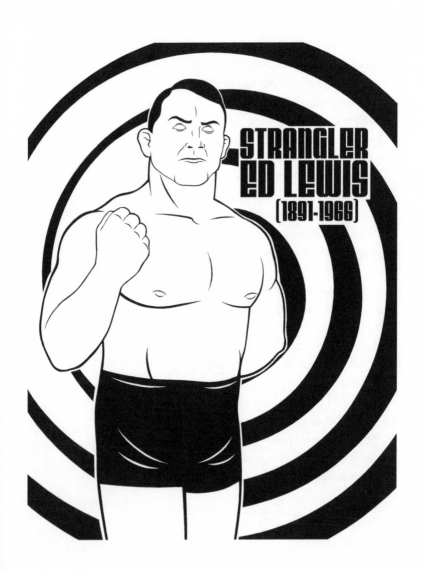

STRANGLER
ED LEWIS
(1891-1966)

BRONKO NAGURSKI BEAT LOU THESZ THAT NIGHT

Tonight, I am in search of clues
on how to be a man, not a man
like my father, who traded his motorcycle
for a job in the plane yards after
my mother left. Before my father tried
telling me wrestling was fake,
we watched men scrap with brass
knuckles and bull ropes. Back then,
a dude could get his jaw broke
calling the wrong guy a fake.
Lou Thesz was a bona fide grappler
stretching men with that toehold
facelock, snapping men's elbows
to protect his championship belt.
My grandfather saw him lose the title
to Bronko Nagurski, celebrated footballer
who stomped men into the turf on his way
to the end zone. Before my father died,
he insisted my grandfather never saw
that match, that men always invent things
when they have something genuine
to say. Today, everyone knows that fight
was fixed. Tonight, I am thinking about
all those shapes Lou Thesz could twist
out of a man's skeleton, and how
some nights that just isn't enough.

TONIGHT, DICK THE BRUISER

I know a dangerous man
will bust some dude open tonight,
a witless victim's body fading
beneath his boots. A bad man doesn't think
he is dangerous—a heel believes in lubricating
the evening in whiskey, in burnishing
dark streaks into the pavement,
tonight. I pretend I am dangerous
some days, pull my hat down low
and swagger like I know that
murderous potential of my thumbs,
that faint difference between an oil spot
and the human heart. Tonight, I watch
Dick the Bruiser take off
his watch before tattooing his name
into a dude's skull with his knuckles.
He is the world's most dangerous
wrestler tonight, and I am older than those
scars I wear under my clothes.
Tomorrow night I will dream
about picking a fight in a truckstop,
a jackrabbit snagged on fence-wire.
The next night, a different fight
in my backyard, a stain in the grass.

BE MORE LIKE SPUTNIK MONROE

It's hard to be humble when you're 235 pounds of
twisted steel and sex appeal with a body women
love and men fear. —Sputnik Monroe

When my father died, he left me a trove
    of video tapes, a warped memorial
for those men he watched with my mother
    before she left for parts unknown,
for those fights he relived once he was laid
    off from the plane yards. We watched
men like Sputnik Monroe bleed the hard way,
    shook our fists as he broke rules
against guys who were easier to cheer.
    He was a bad Elvis: greased back
hair with a shock of white, Sputnik Monroe
    mixed it up everywhere, a rodeo
fistfight, a henhouse tornado. My mother
    picked a fight in an Idaho truck stop
once, stabbed a man's chest with her middle
    finger, then stepped to one side
so my father could fight him in the parking lot.
    Instead, he apologized, guided her
back to the car by the wrist and drove home,
    my mother brooding all the way
back to Seattle. She never forgave ny father
    because Sputnik Monroe clobbered men
wherever he went, sneered at all the fists
    and jeers thrown from the crowd.
Some evenings, as my wife sleeps upstairs,
    I watch my father's video tapes and

imagine what I would have done that day
    if I knew that my marriage depended
on what I did with my hands.

SPUTNIK MONROE
(1928-2006)

JOHNNY VALENTINE WANTED TO FIGHT THE CRUSHER

What can you do other than let the Crusher have his way?
—Chicago wrestling announcer

Men who wrestle for a living,
whose lives are much bloodier than ours,
remain under the lights those nights
they cannot scrap it out. My father said

Handsome Johnny Valentine was a young man
in 1961, elbows poised to puncture a man's skull.
Crusher Lisowski bushwhacked him
before the bell, haymaker and punt
to the gut. When the referee killed the match,
Chicago was primed for blood, my father said—

the Crusher roared over that stadium
chanting for knuckles and thunder, over that wall
of turkeynecks between him and his rival.
Lisowski dragging five men behind him
as he lunged across the ring. Valentine, dashing
fists first at him over the crowd,

a gorgeous promise of agony. Don't worry
about whether or not men fight, my father said.
Worry about what happens when they can't fight.

The Crusher howled for murder, charged
with gravel in his throat, with beer in his belly.

Valentine grinned, punched the air for the Crusher.

That doesn't have to be you and me,
my father said. We don't have to fight.

Zbyszko decided he wanted to win the title and no one had bothered to
teach Munn much in the way of wrestling…Zbyszko was so dominant
the official had to count the fall to avoid a riot.
—Jonathan Snowden, *Shooters: The Toughest Men in Professional*
Wrestling

The part of me that is my father remembers
Big Wayne Munn was supposed to carry
the world championship after wrestling
Stanislaus Zbyszko that day in 1925. I know
that spirit battering itself against my ribs
will give out one day, that a man's body can
fight only so long as his heart understands how.

America knew Munn as a clean-faced
footballer from Nebraska who won
with a half-nelson crotch hold and dump
tackle. The part of me that is my mother
loves how the Polish strongman Zbyszko
double-crossed everyone, how he held Munn
down and forced the referee to count three.
She delighted at the sight of a man's body
in defeat, how he sprawls spent, slackjawed,
eyes shining like cemetery lights.

The part of me that is my father understands
how a man is lured into butterfly clutches,
into chickenwings. The part of me that is
my mother praises dead animals, delights
at shapes the butcher extracts from carcasses.

Whatever part of me that is my own sees
my father's somber expression when I look
in the mirror. Whatever is left of me will be
horsecollar, cattlebrand, a skeleton twisted
into the shape of a cage.

JUDY GRABLE MAKES A LIVING

A woman can't make a living just being a blonde—
although I've heard of a few who have…
—Groucho Marx to Judy Grable, *What's My Line,* 1959

Let's say that a girl's profession
has nothing to do with her body,
that when she changes her hair color
the rest of us will not be harmed.

That vital question: *who are you, will you fight*
                    for what you want?

Let's say the fist is the body, the elbow
is the body, the body is a knee to the face,
a barefoot stomp. When a woman gives up
her body, the way Judy Grable wrestled
every night, someone always gets hurt.

When a comedian asks a girl about her life,
the world laughs or mourns, depending
on how sexy the answers are

to that identical question:
                    what is your life worth?

Judy Grable only answers yes/no
questions, only smiles at inquiries
about sexual contact and happiness.

Let's say the body constantly aches

for release, perpetually moves toward rest
after her constant struggle to answer

the impossible question:

>   *have you ever won?*

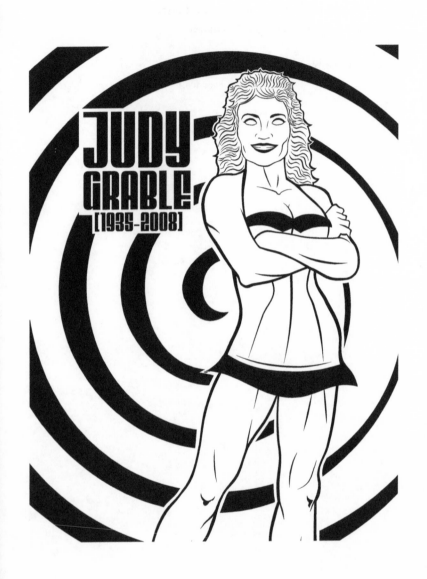

THE NATURE BOY BUDDY ROGERS IS HISTORY

In 1963, his hair bleached into sunshine,
chest bronzed into flame, the Nature Boy
Buddy Rogers parades to the ring
wearing his world championship belt.
He ricochets off the ropes, flying
dropkicks and elbows before grapevining
a man's legs into submission.

Years later, other men swagger through
arenas and television studios clad in starshine
and down, seducing us with muscular
tongues—*listen up slapnuts, it's showtime, wooo!*
A feathery kiss gusting through night
for those pretty girls who come to scream
a man's name in the dark. At a wrestling match

we are all young again, fathers and sons
watching the Nature Boy's descendants fight
under the lights. My mother loved that way
Buddy Rogers taunted his enemies
with a peacock's strut and a lion's sneer
at the monkeys and wildebeest tangled
around his feet. My father loved looking

at photos of my mother. And now I am
in my father's chair where I look at these things
he's left behind. A young man's swagger.
The vainglorious whisper of a motorcycle at dawn.

Oh, if only we both could be in different places.

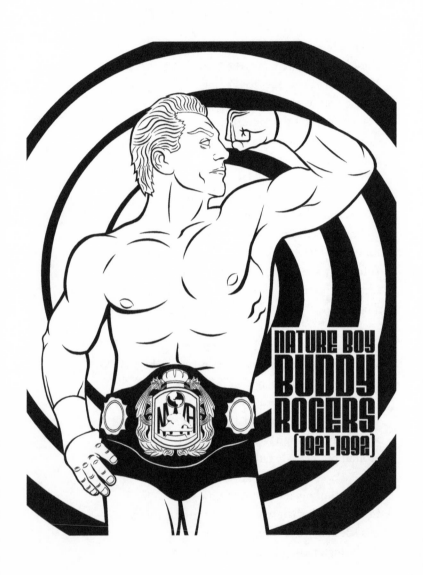

NATURE BOY
BUDDY
ROGERS
(1921-1992)

2

Whatever it takes to win, I will do because that's the way I was raised. And that's the way I'm going to raise my kids, if I ever decide to have any. Take it all. Don't give no mercy. And take no prisoners. —Bad News Brown, World Wrestling Federation

EVERY NIGHT, THE SUPER DESTROYER

A body plunges through the main event
to the canvas, hammer locked, choked,
a death twitch yoked to a mangle of bone.

A wrestling match can be deadly for a man
who believes in pain, who envies cruelty
hidden behind grim faces. No—I'd go back
to being a boy with my father in 1979,

watching that sinister mask and a man
struggling in vain against the claw
holding him above the ground. My father
places his palm in the center of my back,
a tether to the real world where people die
real deaths every night. It's terrifying,

this battle between puny mortals
and that faceless adversary on the other side
of the ring. I pull sorrow into my arms at night,
the way a man pulls another close, knowing
one of them must soon be defeated.

When I watch men fight on television,
it is my father in the grip of the masked man,
it is me held aloft by the face and slammed
heavy to the floor. We are all twisted
into terrible shapes before the final bell.

GORGEOUS GEORGE WAS THE HUMAN ORCHID

Keep your filthy hands off me!
—Gorgeous George Wagner

This drink is for Gorgeous George,
my father said raising a Bud Light to the TV.
The human orchid preened to the ring,
his robe burnished with dewdrop and seaflame,
garish fronds and petals on display.

No man was fit to handle the flower—not
with palm or toehold, collar and elbow
until Gorgeous George purified the stadium
with musk. Tonight I drink for my father,
his arm around my mother, wrestling
matches blaring on television when I was a boy.
He sat alone after she left, the beer trickling
down his chin, the can tipped back for saloons
where a man can sprawl beautiful in the dirt.

The Gorgeous One puffed out his chest,
flexed his arms, flaunting the divine geometry
of a man's body. He scowled at the crowd,
his face imperial, glamorous in close-up.

My father wasn't watching. Don't touch me,
he said as I handed him a beer. That drink
was for all those fights we should have enjoyed.
This drink is for ghosts a man recognizes
on television, for the abrupt lives of flowers,
for all our aluminum cans crumpled
and chucked to the floor.

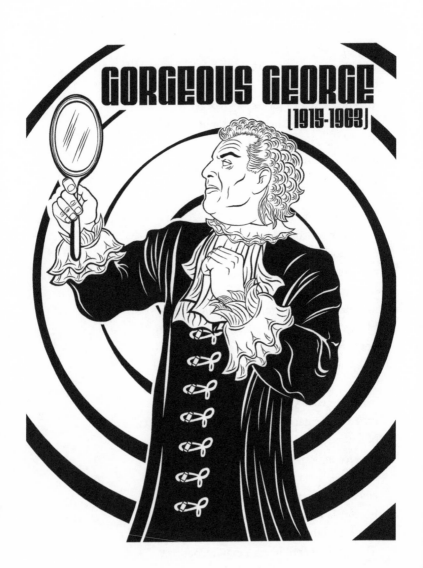

GORGEOUS GEORGE
[1915-1963]

KILLER KOWALSKI AND THE CAULIFLOWER EAR

When I asked my father how a wrestler
sheds fake blood, he said the best thing
Walter Kowalski ever did was break off
that chunk of Yukon Eric's ear. When I asked
if an ear could be reattached, my father
said they called him Killer after he laughed
at all that blood on the canvas.

The cauliflower ear is a brittle condition—
a gnarled badge for men who live by
the fist, who die when they can no longer hear
their names in mouths of women and children.
When I asked my father about my mother,
he explained how Killer Kowalski left
Jack Dempsey gasping on the floor
with a knee to the gut, how he attacked
a talk show comedian with his claw-hold
because he felt like it, how a blow to the head
can bloom thick with gore and cartilage.

Yukon Eric was a babyface for bloodthirsty
crowds, shot himself in a church parking lot
after his wife divorced him. Killer Kowalski
was the most hated man in wrestling,
attacked nightly by ladies with knives
and umbrellas. When I asked my father
about his life before my mother
left us, about those things a man needs
to know about his father before he dies,
he nodded, pretending he couldn't hear.

STAN STASIAK WAS WORLD CHAMPION FOR NINE DAYS

By the time I saw him on television,
Stan "the Man" Stasiak, master of the heart
punch, had become an old man.
My father balanced his sixth Budweiser
on his belly, lamented those days
when Stasiak fought Pedro Morales
for the gold as we watched him
lumbering about the ring, a grizzly bear
wearing mutton chops and a temper laced
with kerosene. He was the oldest grappler
in Portland, ancient hands aching to stop
a young man's heart with a solitary fist.
That old guy was once on top, my father said
staring on a spot on some wall that crumbled
years ago. My father snorted and closed
his eyes, laid there for a few minutes
while old Stasiak clubbed his younger foe:
a series of slow blows, elbow smash,
left hook, haymaker—the television
audience cheered him on. My father's can
tipped into his lap, beer swilling
between his legs and into the sofa.
He shook his head, eyed me without looking
at me—he was world champion. The television
seethed with evil wrestlers swarming the ring,
boots and fists to Stasiak's battered body.
My father laughed, shook his fist
at the television, a beer-soaked whisper—
Men like us should do as good.

BEHIND EVERY MAN IS SENSATIONAL SHERRI

*When he is at ringside, I make sure proper homage is bestowed upon
him and proper respect…All the clothes he wears, every time his boots
get shined, every time that hair is combed, every time that body is
tanned, I am the one responsible for it. I am not a mere manager.
I'm a woman.* —Sensational Sherri Martel

When a woman wears the weather
on her face to expose horses stampeding
through her gory voice, men succumb

to her gorgeous tornado. Sensational or scary,
Sherri Martel waited ringside for so many
great men: Macho Man, the Heartbreak
Kid—even the Honky Tonk Man
with his slick hair and filthy grin
needed a woman to rile him.

My father insisted it was Sherri
who inspired men to be their nastiest
selves. She held men's crowns
as they rumbled for war, mirrors as
they groomed their bodies, their foes
to be bashed over the head
with a country guitar. Back then,
my father believed in solitary men
free from the sway of a woman's fingers,
liberated from that storm of desire.

Back then, I was boy and my father
was a man—all we had was the weather.

BIG JOHN STUDD LOST THE BODY SLAM CHALLENGE

*Take a good look at me New York City and the rest of the world. John
Studd. Seven foot plus nearly 400 pounds of solid muscle and I'm
coming to the ring with a bag of hair that I humiliated Andre with by
ripping it out of his head. I'm also bringing $15,000 because I can't be
slammed.* —Big John Studd just before Wrestlemania 1

After the match, Big John Studd
claimed he still could not be beaten,
that Andre the Giant did not lift him
over his head and slam him to the ground,
the crash reverberating through
our televisions. But we saw him fall
and hated him more for it.

Sometimes a man can't help but deny
those calamities lingering in the body—
a fat lip, a bruised breastbone, a six-pack
of lawnmower beer before breakfast.
After the match, my father nodded
in approval as Studd ducked
out of the ring with the money
as my father nodded in approval.
Later that night he went outside
and threw rocks at the highway,
at all those families speeding
past our building. It's difficult

to bring heartache from where it hides
in the body, where it masquerades
as an angry beard, as bravado spilling

from a man who fell while we watched.
After the match, we were supposed to
hate John Studd because we saw that
body slam. But we knew all too well
that everyone falls, eventually.

BIG JOHN STUDD (1948-1995)

FLOWERS FOR ADRIAN ADONIS

Before he was adorable, Adrian Adonis
was rough. He rode his motorcycle
across the country, wrestled
every man in New York, Hollywood,
Texas—breaking every man he fought
with a knee drop. He wrapped thick arms
around a man's neck, squeezed
until the announcers exclaimed
Goodnight Irene! as bodies crumpled
to the canvas. My father rode
a motorcycle back in the seventies,
an old Indian he gave my mother
when she left us. Sometimes, a boy
is smart to keep silent about things
he finds—secret photos of my mother
astride that bike, her lips peeled
back in a lovely snarl at the Golden
Gate Bridge, at Times Square,
at the Grand Canyon. My father, alone
in his underpants after a double shift
at the plane yards, those photos
gripped in one hand, his forehead in
the other. When he became adorable,
Adrian Adonis was a buffoon,
a man smeared in perfume and eye
shadow prancing through flower shops,
sashaying with a bouquet of posies.
That tough guy who rode his motorcycle
from fight to fight, who fought for the World
Championship, fought for the fun
of beating a man—Good night, Irene!
All that's left are flowers now.

POLAROID OF YOU AND JACK BRISCO

You are 25 in 1973, your arm around
my mother that night in a Texas parking lot.
You wearing a wispy beard and leather jacket
next to your motorcycle, a jackrabbit's grin
as you stare at the camera. You don't see
anything but my mother beside you,

her teeth bared in a sneer or a smile.
That woman's sneer is for me and you,
but her smile is for Jack Brisco, the world
wrestling champion standing next to her.
Brisco, who knocked men down
with an elbow smash, then tied them
in his leglock until the referee stopped
the match. Brisco, who made girls swoon
with his babyface smile and shaggy hair
after beating a man down and strangling
him with his knees. Brisco, giving me
a big thumbs up while his other hand
lingers near my mother's waist.

I wish this photo was mine when you were
alive and willing to talk about riding
with your wife across America, stopping
in every city with a wrestling ring.
You could tell me about that night
Jack Brisco won the championship,
about the day you discovered a woman
can never be owned by a man. You could
tell me a thing or two about those shapes
we all make with our mouths.

This is a cowboy boot planted square
in a man's forehead, a crack of teeth
across knuckles after his marriage ends.
This is a man alone in a fistfight
because every wedding in a wrestling ring
ends in calamity. Love is a gutwrench
suplex, a pumphandle slam to the floor.
This is how a man wrestles with failure.

This is the wedding ring my father wore
on a necklace, a reminder of how
violence feels. This is my father
passed out drunk clutching a cocktail
dress left by my mother. I buried that
garment in the trash when I was a boy.
We never spoke about it. Death
is unconditional, without ceremony.
Love is a trick of memory in the shadow
of a wish. This is the sheen of baby
oil smeared across a man's chest
to remind him how sexy he once was.
This is the familiar taste of blood.

This is my father's collection
of wrestling matches on VHS, mine
after his death. This is a coffee-stained
dress resurrected from the garbage.
This is a man who should have known better.

Because Owen Hart wrestled as the King, as the Rocket,
    as a masked hero called the Blue Blazer.
Because my father watched the Blue Blazer on television
    that night he fell from the rafters and died.
Because we both wanted to believe that a man can fly.
Because there is no such thing as flight, only that
    indeterminate period before a man falls.
Because there is no such thing as falling, only memory.
Because when my father's heart gave out, he fell
    off his barstool and hit his head on the floor.
Because he lived in Seattle and I was in Michigan
    years after my mother disappeared from the map.
Because my father was not a professional wrestler,
    but a welder in the plane yards.
Because a man must do the job he is given.
Because there is no such thing as flight, only desire
    for freedom from home.
Because my father claims to have seen the Blue Blazer
    fall that night on television, his head snapped
    back like a man who has just lost everything.
Because he wanted something to talk about with me
    those nights we sat together watching wrestling.
Because no one saw what happened that night except
    that audience in Kansas City.
Because no one saw what happened that night except
    the bartender who poured him one last beer.
Because it's easy to hurt a man when you don't mean to.
Because the heart is only as strong as the flesh surrounding it,
    the body only as strong as a man can stand it to be.
Because there is no such thing as falling,
    only belief in flight.

That night in Philadelphia, Big Bubba Rogers
was done battling outlaws on the road.
He locked himself in a cell to wrestle
the devil sheathed in leather, the blood angels
in the rafters with several yards of rope.
The Big Boss Man chained the Undertaker
to the cage, rattled handcuffs and nightstick
across skull and wishbone until the dark
prince's eyes rolled back in his head.

After that match, my father called me,
a road trip planned for the two of us—
two men and a station wagon on a quest
for stars, a campfire, a tavern where a man
can meet a woman and not worry about her
whereabouts in the morning. After he died,
I found his notebook, dog-eared, wine-stains
describing the Cow Palace, the Omni,
the Sportatorium—those old arenas
where he and my mother fought for love.

Everything that is dead lies still
before it can return as a phantom.
When evil spirits offer a man a length
of rope, when a man finds a rope looped
about his collar, when panic forms
in the body like Big Bubba Rogers
with that noose tight around his neck,
everything stops. Sometimes a man
finds a way to save himself, sometimes
he just kicks his legs in vain as he rises.

3

You set the stage, my friend. You want to wrestle, I'll wrestle you. You want to brawl, I'll brawl with you. You pick the rules and I'll be there.
—Bruno Sammartino, World Wrestling Federation

BAD NEWS BROWN SAYS YOU DON'T HAVE TO WORRY

You don't have to worry about who you are—whether you're a guy,
whether you're a girl, whether you're black, whether you're white—
because you're going to be black and blue when I get done with you.
—Bad News Brown

You don't have to worry about your guts
or jitters. Whether you're a cock-eyed popinjay
crowing about tomorrow morning's fray
or a beer-bellied sharecropper, soft parts
begging for stiff knees and elbows.
I am a tire iron, a sledgehammer, a shotgun
double-barreled and sawed off

for snail-eyed mama's boys afraid of city
sounds at night, for spineless cockroaches
scurrying into hidey-holes. A man squeezes
his body into a fist, rumbles through subways,
through tenements overrun by alley cats,
by sewer rats, by yellow-bellied jellyfish
cringing at the thunder a man makes
when he speaks. This is the sound of courage,
a lion in my chest chewing down a chicken
necked clodhopper, slobberknocking every
crybaby featherweight. Don't worry

about the different kinds of men you can be.
My name is a mouthful of terrible things
lurking in dark parking lots, under street lights
waiting to clobber any weak-kneed fishwife,
milk-livered footlicker, clown-shoed fraidy cat.

You should be worried.

BAD NEWS
BROWN
(1943-2007)

BIG CAT
ERNIE LADD
(1938-2007)

BIG CAT ERNIE LADD EXPLAINS
WHAT KIND OF MAN YOU ARE

> *Old thunder mouth with his yip yip yip, yawp yawp yawp. Ain't*
> *nobody gonna do this, ain't nobody gonna do that—well you're gonna*
> *suck eggs like an egg sucking dog…You know what they say about your*
> *kind and my kind: we can't stand one another. I'll hurt you for the rest*
> *of your life.* —Big Cat Ernie Ladd

Ain't nobody going to do nothing so long
as he just makes animal sounds. Anybody
can yip yip yip like a toy dog bothering men
on the far side of the yard. You know

what they say about your kind of courage—
body made of straw, head full of grimy birds
cackling for the splendor of his plumage.
After the world knows that quiet punctuating
a man's life, the sky will fill with your yawp
yawp yawp over a pile of tiny bones.

I'm the big cat, mouthful of feathers,
teeth honed on vertebrae and stone.
Ain't no such thing as an honest fight,
just nights you can't spot a man cheating.
Ain't nobody cheating, just death
sporting this beautiful pelt. You know
what they say about tail waggers and
bow wows. I'm the tiger licking his chops
at your front door, the sabretooth raking
claws across your body. Go ahead—sing
your brassy yip yip yip at the night.
See my eyes glowing back at you.

DAVID VON ERICH EXPLAINS THE RULES

I learned a lot about how to face these other guys who break rules [...] I never have been one that really likes rules because rules kind of hinder a man and hold him back. It's really better for me when I don't have rules. —David Von Erich

Rules are what separates a man
from the meat he eats. We can tangle
like beasts, you and me—get all thumb
and eye socket for the henhouse, all
shameless choke hold for the shambles.

When two men go at it all fireworks
and pistol whip, when two dudes
are done jawjacking and collide
all knuckles for claw in the boneyard,
the rules will blur into a flurry
of rabbit punches and country twang,
a spray of blood and flailing limbs.

It's not for love of skyscraper or handshake
or the Texas state flag that I live to be
the babyface. It's that the back burn is good
for the brush fire, that a man can't snuff out
a flame with his fingers without plunging

everyone into darkness. What makes a man
is not the blood staining his chaps,
not his will to go all monkey wrench
and brass knuckles in a feud. I can

pack a boot knife, tie a man down
with bull rope, pummel him with a cow
bell—I can be the bad guy, but we don't
always have to do things the easy way.

CRUSHER BLACKWELL SAYS THERE'S
SOMETHING YOU SHOULD SEE

Have you ever seen a man who has never lost a wrestling match in his life? Have you ever seen a man who can bend bolts? Have you ever seen a man who can bend bars? Have you ever seen a man who can drive a nail through a board with his head? You're looking at him. —Crusher Jerry Blackwell

Have you ever seen a river surge
over capacity, the water spilling
toward your house? Have you seen
a house packed to the ceiling
with that wreckage a man leaves behind
when he dies? You're looking at pain—
a single signal repeated in waves
throughout the body. I can break
the weather across my forehead
because the sky is angry, the ground
with a bellyflop for the debris.

Have you ever seen tears well red
from the deepest parts of a man,
how easily a man succumbs to disaster?
I can gobble up a school of fish, a rush
of cattle, a township in the midwest.
I can swallow everything you desire—
your house, your wife, those highways
running past motels and other women.

I have seen men mangled by mythologies
they have invented for love, for shadows

of absent bodies. I can hold a man
upside-down, watch him struggle before
shivering him into rubble. Look at me.
Imagine all those men I've broken.

CAPTAIN LOU ALBANO SAYS HE IS THE GUIDING LIGHT

I'm like a snake, baby, I move and groove! I can be the guiding light!
I can watch, I can look for weaknesses! I can turn Mr. Saito into a
maniac killer! —Captain Lou Albano, WWF wrestling manager

Don't be a hero if you don't have to—
Be the snake if you need to hurt
someone, the eagle if I tell you to be
a pair of scissors and a tattered flag.
A man can be a pistol, the tip of a razor
for those chumps up in the cheap seats.
Be the beard, wired with rubber bands
and gristle. Be roughneck, bareback
so you can learn to talk to a woman,
hijack her telephone number, her name
if she has one. I am your guiding light

in hours of gloom. I speak with the bygone
snarl of a carnival barker, that salty tongue
spouting from the lips of an exorcist
drunk on church wine. I swallow bees
to hone my bluster, wear my shirt open,
the hair on my chest raked with loco
weed and thistles. A boy is a switchblade
in my pocket, a man a brand new suit
unleashing havoc in the dark.

Listen: you be sabretooth and supernova,
an El Camino charging blind at oblivion.

Be a young stallion, cocksure and lurid
in a fight. Bear skin, bulldozer, broken
bottle brandished in a back alley brawl—
it's your choice. You don't have to
want to be the killer. Just be the killer.

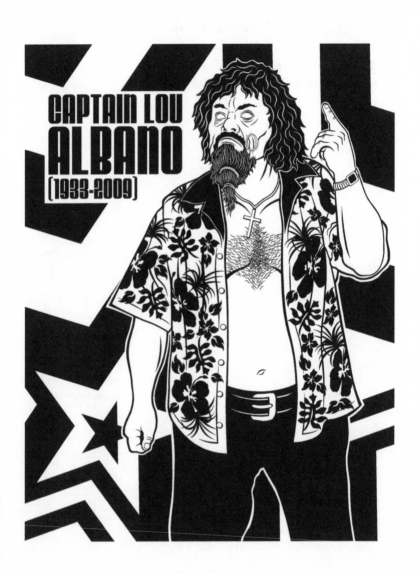

CAPTAIN LOU
ALBANO
(1933-2009)

YOU ARE LOOKING AT DR. DEATH

*You're looking at bad to the bone—Dr. Death! When we get in the
ring, that's when we'll find out who the boy is and who the man is.*
—Dr. Death Steve Williams

You are looking at a man's skeleton,
stronger after being broken. You are seeing
a locked window, panes impervious now
to stone. I am splint. I am bandage. Look at me—
I am the beetle's carapace, the bison's horns.

You are a three-point stance, an Oklahoma
stampede. You are the desperado's secret pistol,
a brigand with a cactus in his throat.
I am looking at an old man who gazes down
at his wristwatch so he won't miss the sunset.

You are beer cans clattering across linoleum,
a ten year winning streak, twenty years broken.
You are broken wishbones dangling from clotheslines.
You are a blood clot.

You are not the sound a body makes
as it collapses to the floor. You are not
those sounds a mouth makes after our bodies
fall apart. You are not a body.

I am a man looking at clouds of bats infesting
the sky, invisible when the moon goes dark.

I am looking for knives long since lost
unsheathed into night. I am looking at the wind.

I am not a boy searching for his father,
not a vulgar prayer uttered by a man
as he wrestles with loss. You are here.
You are not here. I am looking for a place
where we can know exactly who we are.

GORILLA MONSOON, ANYTHING

He was at my mercy. I could've done anything at that point. I could've wristlocked him, broke his arm, broke his leg, broke his neck, done anything. —Gorilla Monsoon after fighting boxing champion Muhammad Ali

I am unyielding like the rain, ferocious
sky blooming wide with dead branches,
with shade. Out at the quiet edge of a fight,
a man cannot know what waits for him to fall.

A boxer is all dashing fists and angry jaw
set for war, reckless hands exploding,
jackrabbits through cemetery grass.

When you can whip any man
in the world, you never know peace—
I am sequoia and antler, a furious wall
impervious to cross or jab, those frantic
movements a fighter makes just before
he discovers the limits of his body.

Too often, a man discovers himself
defeated, upheaved for an airplane spin,
dropped where grave meets sky,
where orchards wither for headstones.

I am whalebone and monument to men
who pick fights with idols then yield
to that grit kicked up by tornados.

I am always the thunderstorm, eroding
all those splintery vows a man makes

when he stands against another man.
I will not just be the rain. I will not
simply be grief. There is always violence.
There is always everything.

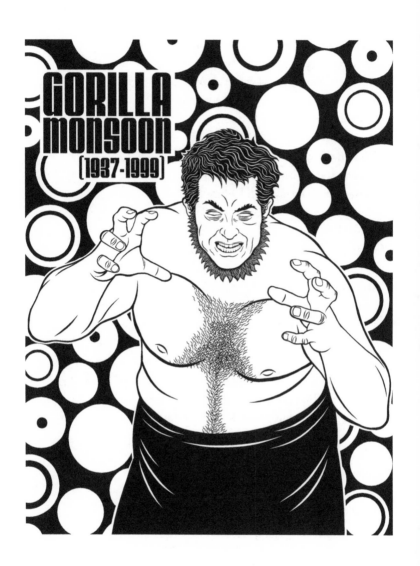

GORILLA
MONSOON
(1937-1999)

THE MISSING LINK EXPLAINS HOW TO BE A MONSTER

Do not look at mirrors. Do not fight
the urge to speak without consonants.
Sharpen your antlers against a coral reef,
fins against an elm tree, hooked teeth
against a fire engine. Do not grow up.

Loosen the needlework that fastens
a man's soul to his bones, his bones
to the names he is called by his children.
Release a man from his skeleton, wrestle him
out of his old skin and let him rise
steaming into night. The referee's hand

slapping the canvas three times is the last thing
a man hears before he must reckon
with his body's malfunction. Be reborn

with a snake's complexion, a caveman's brow.
Terrify the crowd with a prehistoric tongue,
words cracking more like a thunderstorm
than a song for the moon. Don't be afraid

when you awake after a fight, your new body
smeared with blood. Smash your head
into a redwood, a mountain if you want,
until the whole world lay in pieces at your feet.

Try not to grow up to be like your father.
End up exactly like your father.

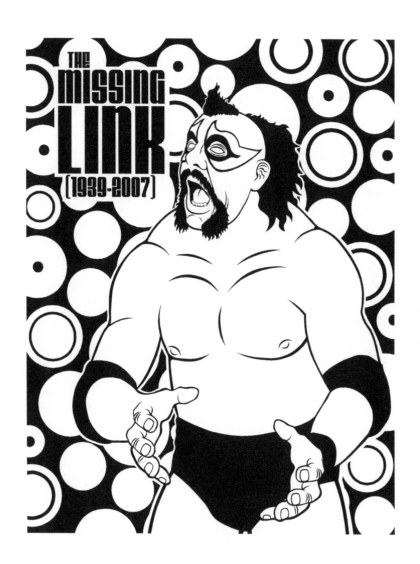

THE MISSING LINK
(1939-2007)

CRIPPLER RAY STEVENS DOESN'T HAVE
TO SAY ANYTHING

> *Surely you would grant that Salvatore Bellomo, if not being your equal*
> *generally speaking, does have assets superior to yours—certainly a little*
> *bit more wrestling technique, would you not say?* —Vince McMahon,
> WWF announcer, to Crippler Ray Stevens

Ask the snake why his mouth is full
of poison, the octopus full of flim-flam
and shade. Ask a flame about tongues
licking for oxygen, the pines standing
courageous against a forest fire.

Ask Ray Stevens about a man's body,
about the poverty of ligaments, the posterity
of knuckles. He will send you ass over heels
across the floor, jam a thumb in your eye
before snapping your thigh bone.

Ask a wrestler about his nicknames,
why he is called after that history
he has forged. The Crippler stomped
a babyface in Frisco, broke the leg off
a masked man in Minneapolis. He will
stroll into your town, climb to the top rope
and drop a knee across any dude's throat.

Ask sorrow why it lodges so high
in the windpipe, the heart why it hurts
those who cling to grief. Ask the Crippler
what kind of man he is. He will show you.

BRUISER BRODY FINISHES THIS THING

I'm going to finish what I started three weeks ago. I'm going to finish it.
I'm going to find me something and I'm going to beat you with it, and
I'm going to beat you with it, and I'm going to beat you with it. We're
going to finish this thing once and for all, fatso. —Bruiser Brody

All I need is a scrap of pine to bludgeon
my way out of a bad spot so I can finish
all those things I've started. As a boy
I finished everything, started fights
because I believed in bloodbaths
with every man in a bar before drinking
to our black eyes in the parking lot.

A knife is a way to finish something.
So is a frying pan, a crowbar, a stabbing
fear in the gut when the lights go out.
A man doesn't hassle with starting, just
tangles fingers in his beard, barks at those
dark spaces where blades wait for a glimpse
of white belly, the inside of a thigh.

A man longs to finish what he can't thrash
with a Louisville slugger, with a tentacle
of chain. This life is not a thing to be finished,
not this busted smile, not this forehead
scarred by scar, not this body left bleeding
in a grimy shower stall. A man must fight
his way out, fight his way out, fight his way
out because he can understand nothing
once this thing is finished.

4

It's hard to explain how you get this great. It's not from eating your Wheaties. It's not from going to bed at nine o'clock and getting up at five. It's from being a man. —Adrian Adonis, NWA Greater St. Louis Wrestling

JUNKYARD DOG ON A SATURDAY NIGHT

It's *Saturday Night's Main Event*—
everyone knows the Junkyard Dog
has a head butt that makes his mother
so proud she dances to "Another One
Bites the Dust." I am fifteen in 1985,
too uneasy to sit near that girl
who draws horses in art class.
Junkyard Dog has vanquished so many
titans with that unbreakable headbutt—
Big John Studd, King Kong Bundy,
Kamala the Ugandan Giant—so tonight,
that soft-bellied sucker doesn't stand
a chance against JYD. I am home
on Saturday night, watching television
instead of stealing beer with my friends,
instead of sneaking an arm around a girl
who might sit behind me in biology.
Junkyard Dog lets that dude punch him
in the face, then blows him out of the ring
with a headbutt. My father taught me
a man never throws a first punch, so I think
about knocking a boy out with my skull,
then making out with that shy girl
from my typing class. Junkyard Dog gets down
on all fours and shows his teeth—chomps
at the dusky stadium air and his mother
shakes her fists. Somewhere that night,
there must have been a girl stuck
at home, maybe watching people dance
on television, maybe wondering about

the precision of her feet, about a boy
who holds one hand to his forehead
when the algebra teacher opens his mouth.

THE GRAND WIZARD OF WRESTLING
CAN MAKE YOU A MAN

The Grand Wizard can take a boy out
of his everyday skin, clothe him in quasar
and chrome, in husks left by constellations
before they rose to Heaven.

The Grand Wizard stands by your side,
cackles in your ear, turns your wishes
into promises, into bare knuckles.

The Grand Wizard conceals a zeal for cruelty
beneath his sinister turban, a coyote's heart
under polyester, those feathers plucked
from phoenix breast and harpy wing.

The Grand Wizard transforms handshakes
into sledgehammers, your shy footstep
into a sexy beast's swagger. Your bow tie
can be a handlebar mustache if you want,
your spectacles an astronaut's suit.

The Grand Wizard can make a man forget
about his old life, the epistemology of loss.
A marriage worn thin, your father's ashes spread
across the night sky reflected on the surface
of a turbulent lake, a story about death.

The Grand Wizard can change your nervous grin
into the lion's jaws, your apologies into the maw
of a crocodile. He sees your future in the stars,

offers you dominion over love and rage
and grief. Just look into the Grand Wizard's eyes.
You will never see his eyes.

*I'm not a first match boy. I'm not a second match boy. I'm a main
event wrestler…you mess around with fire, you're gonna get burned.*
—"Hot Stuff" Eddie Gilbert

Eddie Gilbert is clean cut in 1982,
his index finger pointing skyward in a photo
my father packed away in a box of old
pro wrestling magazines. He leans in
on one knee, his babyface grin kindling
for "Hot Stuff" scrawled in black sharpie
across his silver jacket. He looks
at me for applause and worship
as if to remind me that a boy can't
know what kind of man he will become.

He will be cheered in Oklahoma
until he jams his best friend's face
into a steel ringpost. His manhood
will be defined by the scruff of his beard,
the arrogant sneer of a dude wearing sunglasses
at night. When he outgrows his name,
he will call himself "Hot Stuff," Donna Summer
singing about what she needs from a man
as he enters every arena, as he saunters
to the ring to drive his enemy's head
into the dirt. When he is at his lowest,
he will be King of Memphis, blinding
his foes with fireballs, then flapjacking
them into the top rope throat first.

This is how a man is remembered—
in images he leaves in photos, in that detritus
he leaves after his funeral. Who knows why
a man holds on to those things he does,
what they say about the man he once was?

Hercules descended from Mount Olympus
in 1986, skin of the hydra draped across
his loins, chains swinging heavy about
his neck like Heaven's yoke. My father and I
watched on television that Saturday night
he wrestled for the world championship.

Hercules battled the champion—two titans
snarling and swelling that evening
before they collided knuckles over fist
so my father could forget that grind
of working the plane yards, the weight
of raising a boy alone in a two-bedroom
apartment near the airfield. They battled
until Hercules hoisted the champion up
to snap him in half across his back. We both
hoped to see a new legend begin—Hercules,
a lion's roar in his throat, a stag's hooves
pounding his chest because any man can win
once he learns to bristle with greatness.

We both knew about loss, understood
how Hercules ended up with a boot
to the chin—a loser on his back watching
that atomic leg drop fall from the sky.
Ray Hernandez was from Florida, oiled
down for pose and hypertrophy. We knew
the folly of men who pretend to be anything
other than the men they have learned to be.

PLAYBOY BUDDY ROSE KNOWS HOW MUCH HE WEIGHS

I do not weigh 271 pounds. I weigh a slim, trim 217.
—Playboy Buddy Rose

No one wants to be a bad guy, but to me
Buddy Rose will always be exactly 217 pounds.
My father said I was too short to grow
into a professional wrestler. Every weekend,
the Playboy postured in my father's living room,
half-cocked in glitz and bleach damaged hair.
Not my father's house, but on the West Coast
where men wore tights, grappled for honor
and the love of a good knuckle sandwich.
Before I threw my first punch, before
I understood it's not easy being the bad guy,

my father tried telling me wrestling was fake—
a pageantry of blood and teeth for old men
and wide-eyed children. He told me to study
if I wanted to be a doctor, but Buddy Rose
was a Las Vegas hog flaunting his sallow
physique, jiggling all over in a full-nelson
before tumbling out of the ring headfirst.

Back then, I just wanted to see the Playboy
get his heavy ass kicked. I wanted my father
to show me how a good man makes a fist
out of soft fingers. I wanted to know
what Buddy Rose probably knew back then
as he stomped back to his dressing room—
there is no such thing as a good guy,
only men who look good.

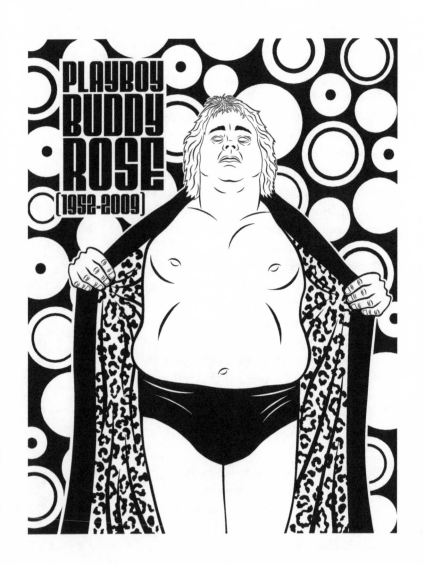

RAVISHING RICK RUDE IS STILL THE SEXIEST MAN

What I'd like to have right now is for all you fat, out of shape sweat hogs to keep the noise down while I take my robe off and show the ladies what a real sexy man looks like. —Ravishing Rick Rude

I am putting my shirt back on
because Rick Rude is still the sexiest
man. He looks right at me as he sheds
his robe, Casanova gyrating, grinding
hips with a gigolo-swivel. My old lady
laughs as he flexes his porn star
mustache, as he taunts the camera
with swelling biceps and a spray
of baby oil. I've never been handsome
like the Ravishing One, never had
the body of a hustler, the whistle
of a coyote. My old lady wanders off
in search of a book or anything smarter
than professional wrestling. I can't see
how a man learns to tie himself up
in lewd pirouettes. My body moves
in one direction at a time, my own
muscles ever aching for that girl
in the next room. Stop calling me
your old lady, she yells. Ravishing
Rick Rude, that wicked Romeo, grins
in the darkness and winks to let me know
that I should keep my voice down.

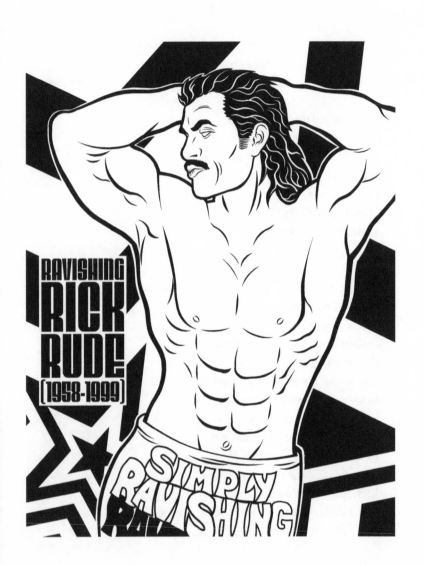

LUNA VACHON IS YOUR SHADOW IN THE DARKNESS

Our history is rich with pain and venom, violence and evil…from this day forward, I will hunt your very breath, I will be your shadow in the darkness. And then soon, very very soon, I will wipe you from this earth. —Luna Vachon

She is butcher and goddess, a throat
full of grackles, a vampire's grin.

She is snake tongue, fistmonger and kill
bride—she is hunger. She is the lightning
eye, the rooster's spurs. Your father
will show you his skeleton one day,
your mother the taint of her blood.

The cemetery is no place for women
slung out in halter tops and bare mid-riffs.
Where there is no such thing as death,
there is only death. She is that ravenous
spirit chewing your name.

She is the lunacy that comes
with grief, lizard tail and owl heart,
a hound driven mad by streetlights
mistaken for the moon. She is the ear
spider, the winter branches.

Her skin is the color of woe. She is
the tombstone, the meantime.
She is a hooked angel excavating
your father with obsidian claws.
She is your mother telling you a story.

THAT NIGHT THE FABULOUS MOOLAH
FINALLY LOST HER CHAMPIONSHIP

The stars were out that night Moolah wrestled
the cowgirl—that's why we came here

to New York in 1984, where alligators crawl
the sewers, where the rat kings skirmish
in alleys. Sometimes, a man can't see the sky
so he invents something to look at.

Moolah the Slave Girl clad in leather
pleats and leopard's claws in 1953.
The Fabulous Moolah now, her pockets full
of dollar bills, flowers perfumed for love
or murder. Moolah—ladies wrestling
champion for twenty-eight years before

this night. We came to see the stars
form new constellations, that neon pop
singer squeaking ringside for Moolah's rival—
the cowgirl blows kisses to MTV,
she-bops under the lights. Her lips glisten

as she slaps on a chinlock, a knee lodged
in the old woman's spine. We remember
what those legends still say—Moolah
was an old beast with a crocodile
cunning, the slipperiness of weasels.

A man feels helpless when he can't help
but root for the wrong woman. Jumping

headscissors, a flying mare. Those bodies
dissolve into tricks of light, the Milky Way
vanishes when the night blooms
dark with loss. That's why we came

here—because Cleopatra still rules Egypt
from the sky, Medusa those undercrofts of bone.
Moolah grabs them by the hair, bashes
their heads together to remind us
who the men really come to see.

JUNE BYERS KNOWS WHAT A WOMAN WANTS

She told me why she was leaving
the only way she knew how,
my mother in the driveway that night—

a story about seeing June Byers
defending her championship in 1955.
Five rows back, my mother watched
two women grapple for the belt.
June Byers, foxy like a rodeo queen,
tied that woman down, arms pulled back,
shoulders popped from their sockets.
My mother stood on her chair
while the champion tossed her rival
into the ropes with an elbow smash
to the neck on the rebound. Spinning
toehold, butterfly stretch, pendulum
backbreaker—June Byers squeezed
a woman by the throat whenever
the referee couldn't see. My mother
squealed with glee as Byers broke
that woman's nose with a right cross.

After the match, my mother looked up
at her father and promised to be a champion
like June Byers, a woman more fistfight
than housewife, more pocketknife than lipstick.
The next day, her parents signed her up
for etiquette school. *Don't go,* I said

into her scent of cigarettes and beer. God,
she said. *Don't be like your father*
before unwrapping herself from my arms,
her taillights vanishing in the dark.

MISS ELIZABETH SAID "OH YEAH"

There are so many ways a man can go
wrong when he wears a cowboy hat,
so many fights he can lose
without the right woman
on his shoulder. I saw the Macho Man
that first time he retired, that night
Miss Elizabeth returned to him.
When I was younger, it was plain
to see—men and women came
together to be separated. My mother
and father fought every night
before she disappeared, riding
for parts unknown. My father has been
alone for decades now that I am grown
with a marriage of my own.
But that night, the Macho Man
hoisted Miss Elizabeth up and held her
high for the world to see her wet
eyes and faultless smile. Divorce
would claim them too—years later
she would be flooded with painkillers
and vodka in another man's house,
but that night she stood on television,
the Macho Man on one knee with that ring
glittering in his fist as the world
waited to hear how she answered.

THE MACHO MAN'S LAST ELBOW DROP

*It's okay for macho men to show every emotion available because
I've cried a thousand times and I'm gonna cry some more. But
I've soared with the eagles and I've slithered with the snakes, and
I've been everywhere in between.* —Macho Man Randy Savage

The eagle doesn't cry. He is too fixed
on majesty to feel bad about gravity's load.
He doesn't know about shady prisons
like that tavern where my father drank
with other worried men perched
at the bar like buzzards, tombstones
mistaken for those creatures
they remember. A man can't change
those scars he wears on the inside,
can't change the names he wears
for the memories of snakes.
A man can't be like the Macho Man,
can't snarl *Oh yeah*—then wrestle
his way back into a marriage or a job
or a heart vanished for parts unknown
decades ago. Worry starts on the inside
as a man climbs to the highest spot
he can find, as he crashes elbow first
back to earth. When whiskey burns
a woman's name into a man's stomach,
when the fist wearies of clenching
nothing but air, a man can point
one finger at the sky, at the stars
gilding his haunches. He can imagine

a secret place where a man can spill
out of his body dank for saloons
where machismo is another word
for worry, another word for God.

5

There's one guarantee in life and that's that there are no guarantees and understand this—nobody likes a quitter, nobody said life was easy so if you get knocked down, take the standing eight count, get back up and fight again…Never admit that you get hurt.
—Macho Man Randy Savage, World Wrestling Federation

CHIEF JAY STRONGBOW KNOWS
ALL ABOUT THE SLEEPER HOLD

Chief Jay Strongbow puts a man down working
a tight sleeper hold in the center of the ring.
That's how he appears in a black and white
photo from the 1970s, a memento
my father left in a cigar box.

But the old Indian could be mourning
for that man slackjawed and falling
limp to the canvas, chin snug in the crook
of Strongbow's elbow. Their bodies
drawn close for that last moment,
a palm laid gentle across the forehead,
a final caress—Strongbow presses
his cheek against the man's crown
and howls at the agony of knowing

this is how a body feels as it grows
empty in his arms. This is that snarl
yoking men to their skeletons,
that snarl entangling us all.
A man cannot contain another's life
in his arms no matter how hard
he squeezes. He cannot know peace
without understanding all that pain
he inflicts on others.

CHIEF JAY STRONGBOW (1928-2012)

WAHOO McDANIEL (1938-2002)

A man can take care of himself
after death. All he needs are his hands
and a new animal to hunt. The sky
sleeps tonight, its voluminous body
consuming what remains: a stone hatchet,
an eagle feather—that leather
strap that once lashed a man
to Chief Wahoo McDaniel, wrist to wrist
with hammer fists and tomahawk
chops, old animals drunk on the scent
of fresh blood and cigar smoke.
We are tethered to ancient things
on the brink, beasts with teeth
yearning for bare chests. We tie
those knots like foxes chew
at their limbs before vanishing.
A man can circle a beast in his arms
and squeeze until it gives in to sleep.
He can wrap legs around his quarry,
an Indian deathlock on the whole animal
kingdom. Now, the antelope gather
drowsy in Spring meadows, rivers churn
thick with salmon and trout.
A man doesn't need his old things
to take care of himself. Let the wolves
take anything left on the prairie.
Let the sky take care of the rest.

WHERE THERE'S BLOOD, THERE'S FREDDIE BLASSIE

In the tavern where my father fell, I find
no bloodstain shaped like my father's body,
no dent where his head clashed
with the floor. The bartender says they talked
about all the men they once watched
wrestle on television—like Classy Freddie

Blassie, hated by every pencil-neck geek
in America. Women swooned for him in California,
the bartender said counting out his till.

Who knows why women do the things they do?
my father said, recounting those twenty-five
people in Japan dead of fright at the sight
of Fred Blassie gnawing on a man's face,
everyone's bodies slicked red.

Twilight calm, tavern hush—dead air
broken by a siren's cry outside,
then a crack like hammerfall,
shivered glass. There is no such thing
as life so long as a man sits alone,
no such thing as death so long
as we say a man's name.

I sit down on my father's stool,
the bartender pulls a beer for each of us.
We talk about the men we used to watch
wrestle until our voices give out.

When the last man has been eliminated
from a battle royale, when Davey Boy Smith
has dumped everyone over the top rope,
do not celebrate for the British Bulldog,
handsome atop the turnbuckles, arms raised,
triumphant over his vanquished rivals.

Some men are not meant to be champions,
my father told me. We cheered for Davey Boy
battling through twenty-nine men, forty minutes
of battering fists and powerslams, the Bulldog
raising men over his head and dumping them
to the ground. My father also told me about fights
with my mother some nights, about mornings
spent nursing a hangover and a busted lip.

Failure is a vortex in the body where a man
can vanish into himself, a curl of sorrow
sluicing over his head. Rule Britannia rang
through the stadium—Davey Boy Smith
tossed the Heartbreak Kid out of the ring
but not to the floor, turned his back,
victorious until he found himself toppled
earthward where the music stopped.

In our living room, my father cracked
another beer and cheered for the Bulldog
as he disappeared from the arena.
We both celebrated Davey Boy Smith
because when a man works hard all his life,
he learns to imagine rumbling for glory, fists
raised skyward toward greatness.

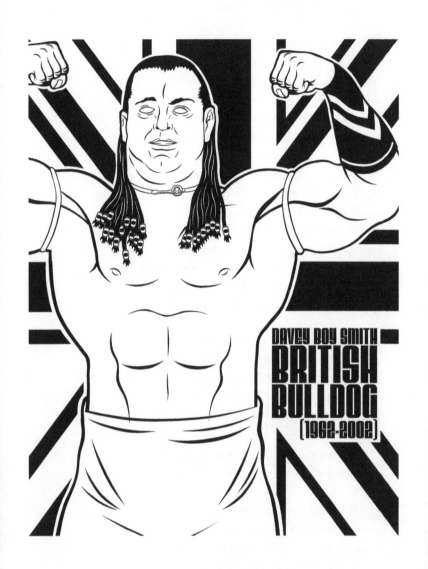

DAVEY BOY SMITH
BRITISH BULLDOG
(1962-2002)

There are so many things I can't understand
without someone to explain a man's capacity
for hurt. My father watched professional wrestling
every Saturday afternoon when I was a boy.
Now that I'm older, I sit in the basement
with his old VHS tapes looking for matches
we used to watch together. Captain Redneck
Dick Murdoch grapples a young buck in Georgia

as Gordon Solie reminds us about Murdoch's
history as a Texas outlaw. Collar and elbow,
fireman's carry takedown into a rigid armbar—
Gordon Solie explains how 'the American Dream'
Dusty Rhodes was betrayed by Captain Redneck,
who hooks a boy's arm, cranks his neck back.
Murdoch laughs and pushes his face into the mat
while Gordon Solie hypes the outlaws' feud—

Rhodes in one corner, finger wagging, hiney
shaking for cheering crowds. On the other side,
Murdoch with knuckles primed to bludgeon
the Dream every night. Murdoch slings a boy
into the ropes, catches him on the rebound
with a headlock, throat punch, brainbuster su-play,

Gordon Solie calls it, then the crowd rumbles low
as Captain Redneck covers the boy for the win.
Somewhere, my father had tapes of Murdoch
and Rhodes tied wrist-to-wrist in Texas, thrashing

each other bloody in Oklahoma, locked inside
a steel cage in Tennessee. I don't watch these fights
because Gordon Solie is not there to interview
anyone after the match, not there to help me
make sense of how natural it is for two men
to hurt one another, even if they don't mean to.

AIN'T NO CAGE CAN HOLD MAD DOG SAWYER

My father had no bedtime stories,
so he told me about that fabled brawl
down south where Mad Dog Sawyer
prowled the backwoods with his mouth
full of rabies, where pain calls the animal
out from beneath a man's breastbone.
Tommy "Wildfire" Rich, decked out
in ivory and gold, that flaxen boy
who filled every stadium with his name,
thrown into that cage with the Mad Dog
to duke it out one last time. They called it

the Last Battle of Atlanta—Buzz Sawyer
furious behind chainlink, Wildfire throwing
elbows and dropkicks, body bejeweled
by blood and rust for the Mad Dog.
That cage was slick with juice,
sick with teeth and hammerfists,
the Mad Dog cackling like fire,
for a man's carcass. I used to dream
about the Mad Dog's yard, a ring of steel
and razorwire where a man can show off
his scars and howl for someone to beat on.
I still see things at night—my father
shirtless in the parking lot, a beer pressed
to his chest, my mother's shadow
astride a motorcycle, rabbits tumbling
headless through the yard.

Pain is a chain of syllables that rises
from the gut and spills from the tongue.
There is no prison like a man's skeleton,
no collar like the bones surrounding
a man's heart as he pushes his belly out
at the darkness, as he batters himself
against the cage, as he wishes
he had different stories to tell.

THE SHEIK LIKES TO HURT PEOPLE

Famous worldwide as the most insane, violent, bloodthirsty competitor
in pro wrestling (and that's saying something), the Sheik was 'hardcore'
decades before anyone had come up with a term to describe his style.
—Professional Wrestling Hall of Fame

What kind of man is this
kneeling on a prayer rug, his hands
outstretched to that savage kind
of deity whose believers eat
their enemies' bodies after a fight?

Take from his palms a lash of starfire,
a kiss of flame—but first, hear the crows
speak in jagged tongues to bodies
buried without ceremony
for the Sheik. He forks a man
in Detroit, punctures a man in Lansing
with a pencil. Tonight, it will be
the wild man's heart that stops
even now that he wears more scars
than flesh. The buzzards know

the kinds of men who pride themselves
on their finesse in butchery, men
who know the aches of war
and desire. Those lamentations
at his passing knife through
the air, a spray of flowers,
a wardrobe of blood-soaked rags.

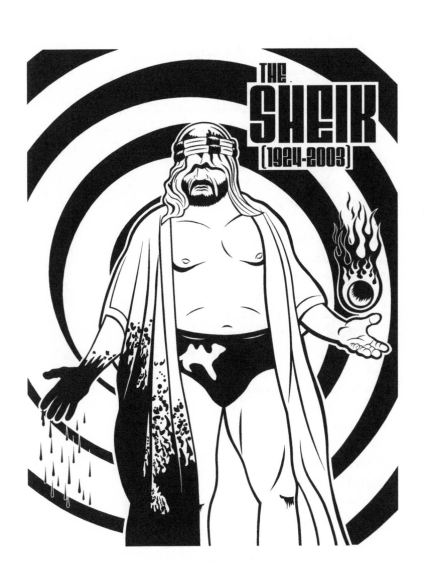

SORROW FOR WOMAN

> [Nancy Benoit] was a breakthrough figure in the sexualization
> of wrestling's femme fatales, so prototypical in portraying
> the charms and treacheries of a woman that her last character
> was known—with an efficiency as stunning as her physical
> beauty—simply as "Woman." —Irv Muchnick, Chris and Nancy

Every night, there is Woman,
snake rattle and wolf
moan in the afterlight.

An angel doesn't have to fall
to be Woman. She can wear
an alligator's skin, war paint
if she wants. From sorrow, a knife
is keened, a shard of memory
wielded to puncture the night

for sparks. Let her be Woman,
not housewife, not goddess.
She can drape you in serpents,
slither about your shoulders.

She can leave with sorrow
buried handle deep in your chest.
Let her be Woman, chainmail
or luminous gown, knuckles
into palm or a finger laid
across your lips. She will remake

the world in her image: spiked
collar and leash, the devil's bikini,
the wolverine's apron. From sorrow,
Woman appears. Let her be the blade
or a brand new animal. Ler her be light
rain, a new word for glory. Let her be.

> *Because you guys are for me, it makes me go fist and fire. I feel you*
> *people in my heart. Without you, the Texas Tornado ain't nothing.*
> —Kerry Von Erich, The Texas Tornado

My heart is half pirouette, half haymaker,
a heavy fist clenched tight around squeals
of boys on horseback, on sugar overload.

My heart thrashes in its cage, a tiny stallion
unbroken for forest fires, a swarm of bees
frenzied in the hive.

My heart is a belt buckle, a dusty leather
saddle, a rusty bicycle chain. My heart
is a dry bouquet of bluebonnets.

My heart is a bruise.

My heart is a question about the lifespan
of a cyclone, how the breeze blossoms
into a hostile wind. My heart
sings along with the tornado siren.

This is not my heart: a motorcycle
crash on a two-lane blacktop, a bluebird
mashed into asphalt. My heart is not
a gunshot wound, is not a broken windmill
abandoned on the panhandle.

No—look at my heart. This lariat braided
from storm tendrils. That herd of cattle
stampeding through cloudburst. My heart
batters itself against the sky's steep pitch.

That wheel of bats is my heart—that rusted
lawnmower blade. My heart spins
until my body turns to mudfish, to night
breath fogging truck windows in rest stops,
to gusts of ash drifting across the highway.

HAWK LEAVES ANIMAL BEHIND

I remember the very first time I heard a bone snap, and I thought
to myself, what a fundamentally perfect sound. I thought to myself,
I could have a future here. —Road Warrior Hawk

Doomsday—the road carves its way through
feathers and pulp, bone discovers itself
jagged into asphalt and a man
chooses between sickness and lightning
when all our yards have gone to weed.
Hawk sticks out his tongue, Animal
grinds his teeth when he speaks.
Raise a boy on gasoline and rattlesnake
bones, so he will dream of the highway.
He will feed on wasps, will swallow
a hornet's nest so the hive can explain
the many strategies of pain. Animal
breaks a man over his knee,
Hawk lifts the carcass over his head,
heaves it off a suspension bridge.
The Road Warriors bludgeon their way
across America—Hawk batters a man
with a washing machine, Animal
brandishes a tire iron and a crossbow,
Hawk wraps his arms around a pine tree,
a cloud of splinters and crows.
Sorrow is a difficult creature for a man
to battle, a two-lane blacktop his substitute
for grief. Animal beats up a Volkswagen
Beetle in a deserted rest stop, Animal
beats up a mountain with an axe handle.

Animal punches out every cowboy
in every tavern—when he goes to slap hands
with his partner, all he has is the road.

13.

After the dinosaurs fell
asleep, after those terrible lizards
began their slow decay into mythology,
Andre the Giant was there to cradle
their bodies in his soft hands and weep.

24.

Andre the Giant wrestled the Earth
into a globe, carved his name into the ocean
floor with his pinky to remind the whales
who taught them to sing.

32.

Andre the Giant was a village.
Then he became a dragon.
Then he became an army.
Then he became a king.
Now, he is the wind.

40.

A man can't bodyslam Andre the Giant
unless he's worthy of slaying a monster, unless
the giant decides it's time to lie down.

58.

Andre the Giant stole fire from Heaven,
hid it in his mouth, fed it to monkeys
one lick at a time until they learned
to pronounce his name.

67.

Before there were boys with magic
beanstalks, with slingshots or singing
swords, Andre the Giant brawled
with sooty angels, volcanoes spouting
from where he buried their hearts

75.

Andre the Giant scaled the Empire
State Building with Marilyn Monroe
in one hand, Cleopatra in the other.
They marveled at how small we are.

81.

Andre the Giant once cracked the sky's ribs.
Then he was thunder churning like trout.
Then he was an avalanche of fists and knees.
Then he was a fire burning through the forest.
Then he was a tidal wave seething offshore.
Now, he will not be a metaphor.

93.

When Andre the Giant pitched a man
over the top rope and out into the crowd,
he aimed at the moon.

100.

A man never tells a lie, always treats a promise
like his mother's name. Andre the Giant
once threw a silver dollar across the Potomac,
hit a buffalo in the eye and killed it as it grazed.

116.

Andre the Giant drank three bottles of whiskey
and grappled with the Devil in a bingo hall
in Memphis. Then he invented the blues.

125.

On television, Andre the Giant grinned
with a mouthful of shark's teeth. He devoured
mortal men ten-at-a-time, laughed and spit
their bones into our living rooms.

137.

Andre the Giant was a Frenchman.
Then he became an ogre.
Then he became a movie star.
Now, he is the constellations.
All of them.

ANDRE
THE GIANT
(1946-1993)

6

The undertaker is always closer than you think.
—Paul Bearer, World Wrestling Federation

PAUL BEARER SAYS WE ARE ALL ALONE

O Undertaker, I've been sitting all alone in the darkness of
my funeral parlor. —Paul Bearer, WWF wrestling manager

O undertaker, there are only
so many deaths a man can enjoy
when agony glows lonesome
in the body. There is only one way
for a man to die when there is no one
to watch his shadow flicker miserable
against the wall. O undertaker—
a man can't survive a fireball,
can't burn alive without collecting
scars where he longs for a kiss.
A man can't smolder like he used to
now that we have so many new words
for love—gravel, epitaph, fiery
elegies for everything we will one day
leave behind. O undertaker—I've been
waiting for my father's funeral,
for that day his passing will be
marked by a woman's fists
against his casket. There is only
one way for a man to cry, one way
for a man to say goodbye.
O undertaker—most folks believe
in that fire seething beneath
a man's breastbone. In the evening
when you burn the body, I will step
into the crematorium and find myself
unable to bear the flame.

PAUL BEARER (1954-2013)

A BOX FOR YOKOZUNA

From the dark rises Yokozuna—
sumo king with a belly full of thunder,
a hunger for pushing men off
their feet, into the earth. His eyes
grow wide at the thought of a coffin,
that luxurious interior, that grim
receptacle for hair and bone.

It's that push a man's body makes
against other men that defines how strong
the flesh can be. It's that push against
Yokozuna that marks the limits
of a man's body. Death looks smaller
when viewed from a distance, more
insidious from the inside of a box.

Yokozuna looks bigger as he pushes
a man down, as he mashes a skeleton
beneath his buttocks. It's that thump
thump against ribs that reminds
a man of dark spaces that push
in on him when he is alone.

Yokozuna claps his hands, purifies
the ground with a stomp, the air
with a handful of salt for dead men
suffering in a world without sleep.
Somewhere there is a bed for each of us,
a box that will not open no matter
how hard a man might push.

A MAN IS NOT AN EARTHQUAKE

I'm not the shark. I'm not a fish. I'm not an avalanche. I'm a man.
—"Earthquake" John Tenta

Call a man after a force of nature, a natural
            disaster when disaster is another word
        for that wreckage he carries on his bones.

            Call him a catastrophe when he needs it
                most, an avalanche heaved skyward
    and down across all our chests. Never second guess

        the weight of a man's name. The earthquake
    knows its seismic limits, its capacity for ruin
            so far from where a man falls hard

                on the inside and hides his injuries
                    behind a six-pack of beer and
        a punch in the arm. Call a man for the shape

            his body makes under the lights,
        for that species of animal he pretended to be
                before we discovered that calamity

        lurking in his medical charts. Call him out
            for all those tragic things he has done.
    Hide from the back of his hand, that cruel mark

        he will leave on your carcass. This life
            is an accident, a pile of broken stones.
    Men are prey to those shadows of everything

they have lost in life. Call a man whatever name
        feels best in your mouth—call him injury,
  emergency, father. Call him home.

EARTHQUAKE
(1963-2006)

WE DO NOT WANT TO BELIEVE THERE IS A PLACE IN HELL

*ATLANTA, June 26—Chris Benoit, a professional wrestler known as
the Canadian Crippler, killed his wife and 7-year-old son in their house
in Fayetteville, Georgia., over the weekend before taking his own life by
hanging himself with a cable from a weight machine in his home gym.*
—The New York Times

We want to stop wondering what makes a man
hurt his family, how we ever cheered
for a monster. We want to suspend our disbelief
in television violence, in the frailty of animals' bodies.
The wolverine is a sensitive fiend, ravenous
for bones and back teeth. Winter cannot know
what the animals sing about as it settles,
drowning the woods in silence. The cruelest beasts
love their brood, even if only a mouthful.
Imagine a love turned inside out and hung
from the edge of the moon. Imagine songbirds
broken in Spring, their fiery bodies glittering
like broken beer bottles, like rain puddles.

Somewhere, there is a place for all of us
to figure out what evil things we are
capable of believing. We want to understand
the distance between love and fury, the damage
a brain can do to a body. If a man cannot fathom
the sky's brim, we cannot distinguish the sun
from a forest fire, a murder of sinister birds from
the Devil's tongue. We want to believe
a wolverine can fly. We need to believe in men
who are good no matter where they die.

MR. PERFECT IS WHAT HE SAYS HE IS

Never before in the World Wrestling Federation has there been a man like Mr. Perfect, somebody who has it all from top to bottom. Muscle symmetry. All the things are in the right places:the blond curly hair, the blue eyes…I am what I say I am, and I say I'm absolutely perfect.
—Mr. Perfect Curt Hennig

I remember my father in heroic postures,
that chiseled shape defying every
slow corrosion. A statue can inspire a man
to flex his arms and admire muscles long
since gone slack. Before he was Perfect,
Curt Hennig was a gap-toothed babyface
wrestling alongside his father Larry
the Axe in Minnesota. Ain't nothing
wrong with a boy wanting to be
like his old man, my father said
as the Hennigs watched each other
get beat up in the far corner.

Remember Mr. Perfect as the man
he became: that flawless athlete shining
on television, a man dazzling his father
with suplexes, with deathlocks.
My father knew how the heart works
to repair itself despite the hangover
aching in his belly. Every man's body loses
its symmetry, hurting in invisible places.
His body cannot remain perfect,
must remain perfect until the world stops
hurting, until the statuary becomes an ossuary
no matter how we imagine it.

After the empire fell, after the fires
left scars over backs of foxwife
and fisherman, Rikidozan invented
professional wrestling for Japan,
swallowed the atomic bomb, then
devised a new word for faith.
After my mother left us, after
my father dreamed of starting over
in a new place, the way Rikidozan
appeared in Japan with karate
chops and arms that grapple
men to the canvas for a quick one
two three—Rikidozan, with thunder
in his hands and sun fire to forge
new names for virility, for honor.
Rikidozan with eagle claw. Knife
hand. Dragon's tongue. Rikidozan
using the deadliest parts of a man
to breathe life into battered bodies.
My father watching television late
into night until every grappler faded
into static and snow. My father
tinier in that dark room than he is now
in death. Rikidozan devising new names
for manhood. My father proclaiming
that professional wrestling is fake,
Rikidozan explaining that authenticity
doesn't matter when a man
needs something to believe in.

1.

A man can stand with both feet touching
the ground until his legs no longer reach
that far, until the ground disappears.

2.

Giant Baba stands six feet ten inches tall, taller
in Japan. It doesn't matter how tall you are.

3.

A man can hold a woman, can't stand to lose
her to the heart's wreckage. His body will fall
apart one day—a rock crab's chassis stripped
clean by seagulls, a dandelion gone to seed.

4.

Giant Baba stands over seven feet tall.
When he lifts you over his head, you will be
eight and a half feet above the ground.

5.

A man can stand for anything when seen
from below—fatherhood, majesty, satisfaction
after conquest. In the end all men are seen
from above—patch of lawn, chunk of stone.

6.

Giant Baba towers above your house,
dangles you by the ankle. Your life
looks so small from the sky.

7.

A man and a woman can wrestle together
in the same bed. A man and a woman
and a marriage can brawl all night.

8.

Giant Baba looms dark against the stars, back
blotting out the Milky Way, arms cradling you
and your family history. Listen to his mammoth
heartbeat, war drum, earthquake. Just listen.

9.

A man can stand naked in a foreign country,
can search for meaning in strange tongues. He tries
to find himself in stories about famous battles,
about giants. It doesn't matter where he stands.

10.

Giant Baba's body is made of girders
and mastodon bones. When you stand outside
to look at your house from new angles,
when you think of how your father died,
the giant will be there to catch you.

WHERE BOBO BRAZIL LIVES

*Do you know where I come from? I come from a little small town
by the name of Benton Harbor, Michigan. Do you know what
street I live on? I live on Tough Street. Do you know where I live?
At the very bottom of that street. But I don't go around bragging
about how tough I am.* —Bobo Brazil

You can learn a lot about a man
by knowing where he comes from,
a town where bowfins once prowled
for crayfish, ospreys preening in the reeds.
Here is a washing machine, an old tractor,
boarded up strip malls and factories spread
out on a four-mile grid. Where I come from

a man knows the color of his skin,
like he carries the weight of his knuckles,
the velocity of temper. Boys strike lightning
to build a fire. Girls spark cigarettes to life,
bloom red in the dark, then exhale
smoke to cloak all our worries about
where anyone lives. You can learn a lot

about a town by the contours of a man's body:
cauliflower ear, split lip, bruised tailbone, fists
all raised toward Heaven. We know the street
fights and flowers, heartbreak and kidney
punch—then a man crying on the lawn

surrounded by police radio chatter. Everyone
needs someone to root for, someone to lift
them up. Everyone knows how tough

we are in this neighborhood. And beautiful.
Now that's something to brag about.

EDDIE GUERRERO'S LAST FROG SPLASH

Don't forget my motto, homes—I lie, I cheat, I steal.
—Eddie Guerrero, Latino Heat

When Eddie Guerrero feels
good, he flickers and jukes
in the ring before climbing
to the top rope to frogsplash down
across our chests. He steals our cars,
our wives, then flashes a smile
that way the alligator invites
the world to admire his teeth.
A man can't help but wrestle
with how his heart cries *Life!*
Life! then wrangle a second chance
at death with a water moccasin
in his mouth. Like a jagged kiss,
like the swift tip of a bullwhip,

a man can vanish in the dark
as he imagines a different life
while Eddie Guerrero wallops us
with a beer can, with a cowboy boot.
He shows his teeth when he growls
our names, the way a man confesses
love when he's worked so hard
to conceal all he's done—we cry

Life! Life! Sometimes a frog dies
trying to fly the only way he knows.

The sky takes so much from us—
breath from our lips, those animal sounds
we make at funerals. We know those cries.
We know how tadpoles feel.

LATINO HEAT
EDDIE GUERRERO
(1967-2005)

GENE KINISKI SAYS IT IS NOT THE END

It is not the end. It is the beginning. I have started a job and I
am going to finish it. When you spend a dollar to see Canada's
greatest athlete, you will get a ten dollar value. —Gene Kiniski,
interviewed after his last match, age 61

This is not an old body, it is a spark
soaring since the first flicker made by flint
and stone. This is a caveman's wish,
a hungry roar for flesh where the ocean
once seethed for shore. When you spend
your life stretching men out, twisting
legs off, yanking arms free of shoulders

until all that's left is the meadow
of his bones, you will understand
the wisdom of pain. It is not ground
for you to trample, it is a black sky
descending sudden on you like
an eagle's claws, an airplane wing,
like all those tears shed at funerals.
When a man worries too much
about the wind's cruelty, he forgets
he can be the bird riding an updraft.
He can be the hurricane, if he wants to.

You can be a mother who tells stories
about the boys we should have been.
You can be a boy and I will remind you
I am not your father. I am flame.
I am gravel. I am ocean and airstream.

I'm a man. This is only the beginning.

7

When I get to Heaven, I'll want to fight.
—Rowdy Roddy Piper

There were two bad people. One was John Wayne and he's dead, brother. And the other one's right here. —"The American Dream" Dusty Rhodes,

Hard times are when a man makes a living at not making a living in America.

Hard times are when a man's body finds itself out of work so it stops working.

Hard times are when a man makes a lightning bolt with his heart, electricity pulsing through all our bodies after he's been planted in the ground.

Hard times are when the electricity lingers in the air long after the shock has worn off.

My father spent most of his life working, so much of his life dying, his whole death trying to work again.

He said there are two kinds of men in this life: one wears a six gun on his hip and the other whips out a blindfold and tells him where to shoot.

He said this before he died and now that's all he says.

Hard times are how for every good man working a 40-hour-a-week job, there is another man working that same job for more money.

Hard times are how for every good man, there is a bad man who has done his best to be good.

My father said there are no good or bad men, only ghosts who haven't yet earned their flesh.

He said there are no such things as ghosts, only men who step outside at night and wonder what it's like to walk on the moon.

Hard times are knowing someone planted a flag on the moon, a
   beacon in the sky for those who don't believe in God.

Hard times are when the night sky is overcast and when you
   look for God, all you see are the street lights reflected back at
   you.

My father carried his heart in his lunchbox, my mother's name
   where his ribs came together, a cathedral over his softest
   place.

My father taught me about America, where a man can pull
   himself up by his bootstraps and achieve anything he wants.

My father taught me about America, where there are no actual
   bootstraps, just boots pressing down on the back of a man's
   neck, on the backs of a man's family.

Hard times are when a man discovers the majestic peaks on the
   horizon are just a cardboard cutouts of mountains.

Hard times are when a man discovers the lighthouse on that
   distant shore is just a sad kid playing with a flashlight.

Hard times are the shipwrecks, the drowned crewmen, a sailor
   without an oar, all the debris a man mistakes for treasure
   scattered on the ocean floor.

Hard times are when a man mistakes his body for debris, his
   life for a shipwreck, his family for the jagged rocks on the
   shore.

My father died by himself but he still visits me every evening.

He says hard times are when a man discovers he isn't living
   anymore.

He says hard times are when a man wants to have faith in
   something other than the body that has failed him but
   there's a funeral bell ringing in his ear.

He says he is still haunted by the shadow of the woman who
   left him.

The last time he saw her in the driveway, she straddled his
  motorcycle and rode it off into the night.

The last time he saw her in the harbor, she held a torch in one
  hand, a stone tablet in the other, and she refused to look at
  him.

Hard times are when your father's ghost talks to you and
  doesn't make sense.

Hard times are when your father's ghost talks to you and you
  haven't yet figured out you can hear him.

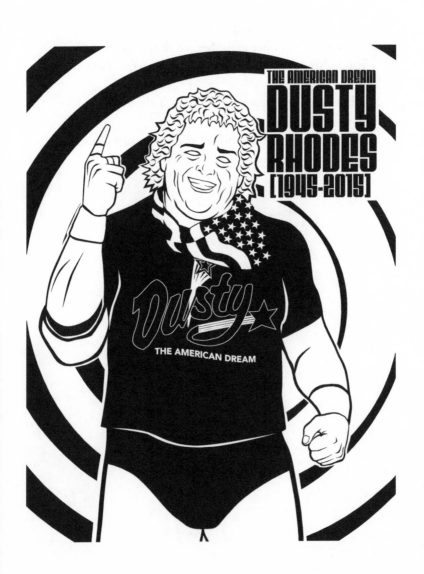

ASK TERRY GORDY WHO HE IS

I am not a half-nelson or head scissors,
not any shape a man makes with his body
as he battles out of the clinch. I am the red
sky settling on the Tennessee valley,
whole herds of cattle suddenly in flight.

I am not the chicken wing, never the butterfly
or clover leaf. I am knuckle and jawbone.
My boots are stitched from panicked leather,
from the lariat's wistful flight. I am the longhorn
mutilation, the butcher's apron at day's end.

One day I will be the winter lavender,
the flock oblivious to skyscraper and flight path.
You will be the tavern after hours, the tattoo
parlor left inkless after a funeral. I will be the boat
lost in the Gulf of Mexico, you the ocean.

Don't call me omoplata or anaconda
choke—instead make those grunts of oxen
at one with their yoke, that rattle
hovering over a dead man's lips.
I will always be the graveyard romp,
boot stomp and mouse bones. The whisper
of lightning. The bullwhip splinter.

Ask the ambulance driver who I am.
You already know my answer.

FIVE COUNT FOR KING KONG BUNDY

When I get in the ring, I always want two opponents, and when
I have an opponent, they get a five count. —King Kong Bundy

1.

When King Kong Bundy wrestled
a man to the ground, he refused a three count,
made the referee count to five to show
everyone how easy he could wreck a man.

2.

At sixteen, sneaking out at night,
I left my window unlatched in case
my father was on the couch watching
wrestling on television when I returned.

3.

Some evenings my father appears in my room,
his spectre with the weight of everything
he lost in his life: wife, job, house—you
can't move when the dead hold you down.

4.

When I was a kid, my father used to warn me
to be good or King Kong Bundy would
appear one day and squash me flat. I never
learned what he meant—be good is all he said.

5.

My father is dead and I watch wrestling at night
to remember him. When the screen goes dark
I sometimes glimpse his reflection next to me.
I count to five. Then he is gone again.

KING KONG
BUNDY
[1955-2019]

REMEMBER PENNY BANNER

*If I had to be remembered one particular way, I would want to be
remembered as an athletic, good looking woman, full of life, that likes
to have fun. That's what I'd like to be remembered as. And I would
also like to be remembered as the first AWA Ladies Champion.*
—Penny Banner

In a wrestling match, the self vanishes
for a ravenous fury, a rag doll swept up
and lost to desire's tornado.

In old photos I flash a siren's grin,
recline in leopard print and fur—
then dropkick a girl, drill her
in the teeth with a rabbit punch and snarl
at the referee. At night, the body moves

through car chase and cocktail party
until sunrise. In a fight, the body
unsheathes itself for the slaughter, for agony
is gorgeous as it drips from the face.
I've kissed rock stars, tangled with rodeo
queens—subdued them all with a headlock
takeover and the memory of a whirlwind

of lips and elbows, a woman rumbling
for glory under the stadium lights.
I am bombshell and knockout, champion
of the mat. Look at those old photographs,
at that bikini line and the curve of my smile.

See my leg scissors and hard knees
because the fight is not desire, not prelude
to death. I am all of these things.

Remember me.

MAE YOUNG HAS ALWAYS BEEN THE HEEL

Anybody can be a babyface, what we call a clean wrestler. They don't have to do nothing. It's the heel that carries the whole show. I've always been a heel, and I wouldn't be anything else but.
—Mae Young

Anybody can be the tulip, the nightingale,
cherry blossoms wafting across orchards
in summer. It's easy for a woman to cock
her hip and smile at boys, for a girl
to glimmer in rhinestones and lipstick.

Screw that—I've never seen a woman
I couldn't lick, never a man I couldn't
hammerlock and stomp into the canvas.

Forget flowers, following animals naked
and pale through groves to gravestones.
Give me a cigar and a pair of trousers,
zipper up the front and rolled at the cuffs.
We can go down to the waterfront, pick fights
with longshoremen, with sharks.

Anybody can get married, start a family
and dance to songs on the radio.
I am the alligator's smile, perilous
and sexy like a cocaine spoon,
like a barbed wire kiss. I fight in a cage

because some nights I am showered
with beer bottles and old vegetables.
Other nights men seek shelter
from my elbows and knees. It's easy
for stadiums to rally against me, for cities
to curse my name all night. I'll always be
the heel, desire and violence flickering

together like a house and a fire,
like your house and my fire.

MAE YOUNG
[1923-2014]

*Find the toughest ten wrestlers that you've got and put them on one
side of the ring. I'll stand on the other side and one at a time, I will
defeat them…I'm tough and one thing that I have is my famous
heart punch. I love to hurt people.* —Ox Baker

This is a fist to make men
remember how soft they are
where their skeletons recede
into guts. Make them give up
claim on the ghosts of desire—

hospital bedsheets, decades old
songs on the radio and a bruise
marking that spot in the anatomy
where kindness once roosted. I punch
all the bodies dark, one by one,
mash the night into men's chests,
their organs into cemetery wine.

The great heart puncher now waits
for the finish, knuckles crackling
for the body's eclipse, the final
haymaker, blunderbuss at the end
of the universe. When the flesh is

at the brink of defeat, when
the physique verges on collapsing
into a heap of brittle hair and bone,
when the world witnesses my hand's
velosity as it streaks toward your center,

don't fear what will happen to you
in the afterlife. Be afraid for
what is about to happen on Earth.

Tonight I am watching Bruno Sammartino lose
his championship again, that era's greatest hero
When the match was over
fallen to the evil Russian Bear, Ivan Koloff.
Both wrestlers were famous for their bear hug,
Sammartino thought he had lost
but tonight there are just knuckles and boots
until the end. The bear hug is boring
his hearing because he couldn't
my mother says, there's nothing exciting
about watching two men hugging
hear the crowd's response
when they could be fighting, nothing electric
about a desperate embrace where a man holds on
but really it was the world
for his life or someone else's life, depending
on the fight and who he is holding on to.
that watched him lose the match
Is this what my father thought when he watched
this match by himself? Are these my mother's
and found only that still hush
spectral words overlapping the announcer's silent
commentary? Or maybe this is grief talking
like the air between a bird and the ground,
me through the match because who knows what
there is left for a man to hear in the quiet
like the stone crying a man's name
night where he discovers himself alone
with his ghosts. Tonight there are no bear hugs

where his body lies, like the breath
  and I watch the bad guy win again, then rewind
  the video to watch once more and Oh, father.
of God hanging solemn over everything.
  Oh, mother. If only we knew how to listen to
  the world. If only we had something to listen to.

DOINK THE CLOWN CLOWNS AROUND

Paul E. Dangerously and everyone in the ECW says, "this is no circus." No, circus it isn't—but I can clown around and I can still kick your ass. —Matt Borne

A man walks into a bar
because it's funny and a man isn't
a clown just because he dresses like one.

Tonight, fear is the costume: fright
wig, lipstick, a goon's complexion
for childhood gone cockeyed.

A man walks into bar, sucker
punches you, then sits on your stomach
and recites dirty knock knock jokes
until closing time. It doesn't matter

who's there—the punchline is always
a face full of seltzer and a floppy shoe
across the bridge of your nose. It's funny
how the difference between man and clown
comes down to the color of his nose
and the size of his squeeze horn.

A man walks into a bar. He buys you
a drink and follows you back to your apartment.
In the morning, he has harvested your kidneys
and your cat is pregnant.

A man dressed like a clown is still a man.
When the man collapses, the clown is all
that remains. Surprise—it's not funny.

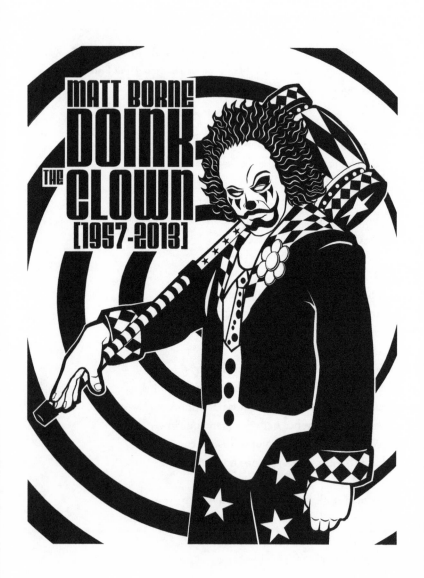

MATT BORNE
DOINK
THE CLOWN
[1957-2013]

HARLEY RACE AND THE BODY SLAM

*I got him in the position and brought his head full through all in
the same motion. It's when those pauses come in, and that weight
is allowed to come straight on you, that you get hurt.*
—Harley Race, on body slamming Andre the Giant

The fights have been plentiful
since my father died, battle-scarred bodies

hostile in shadows, violent on television
because a fight never finishes

when the bodies stop moving, no more
sweat and carnage where fists are inseparable

from the bruises they make, from the bodies
they leave in their wake, like Harley Race

was the toughest man in professional wrestling—
he made a body slam beautiful, the way

he could lift a giant over his head and down
in one fluent motion, a chevron of geese flying

southbound over the house, the ocean
gently massaging the shoreline

back into itself, flesh turning to flowers
to feed the flesh, because he once said that

it's important to keep the body moving,
that it's when you stop and let the weight

sit on you that a man risks being hurt,
so I cannot apologize for the carnage

continually spreading across the floor
of my room each night, the fists flailing

at every wall and shadow, the quietude
where grief blooms red and wet.

I DREAM OF CHYNA FIGHTING

Chyna flexing her arms ringside, Chyna knocking
a dude out with brass knuckles, Chyna bashing
a man with a chair. I dream of a beautiful scowl
like the slivered moon gone dark above my house

where there were once birds, once a bright night sky.
My father watches pro wrestling in my living room
at night even though the television is off, even though
he is long since dead and buried. He watches

Chyna bludgeoning a man with a cast iron pan,
with a stew pot. Chyna lifting a man over her head
and tossing him into the grave. I dream of my mother
in the kitchen after dinner—she washes the dishes

while I dry. She touches my cheek with wet fingers
promises to one day teach me how to be alone.
When I wake up, my face is still wet as I think
about Susan B. Anthony entering that voting booth,

Marie Curie and her Nobel Prize, Joan of Arc talking
to God. Chyna with her championship held high
over her head for all of us to admire. Chyna breaking
out of every cage, steel bars buckling in her hands.

Not Chyna but her ghost. Not Chyna but the night
my mother left while I was sleeping. My mother
looking for a fight with a mop and a trash can
as the world cheers her on. My mother with the gorilla

press slam and face buster and my name in a whisper.
Above my house is a flickering signal in the shape
of a woman. Chyna cracks her knuckles and my father
and I are outside still looking for the moon.

QUESTIONS FOR RODDY PIPER

> *Just when they think they got the answers, I change the questions.*
> —Rowdy Roddy Piper

If a man falls and no one is
around, does he make a sound
like a car crash in the distance
or like summer's last wheeze,

> the final gasp of bagpipes
> on the green? Have you seen
> the light go out of a man's eyes
> just before he is hit by a fist

or a hammer or a coconut?
You can wrap a chain around
a man's neck, collar him
to a forty-hour work week

> and a thirty minute commute
> each way along with the poor
> saps who don't have a name
> for what they do besides work,

but what is there a man can't do
with his hands when there's no one
around to fight? When there's no one
left to leave looking like bruised fruit,

no one to wonder what it means
to be a man like my father, spoiling
for a fight while the rest of the world
is asleep? When the darkness lifts,

the lights will shine on him so bright—
can you see the shape his body leaves
on the ground? Do you recognize
the shade of his absence?

Can you imagine how dark
the world is without him?

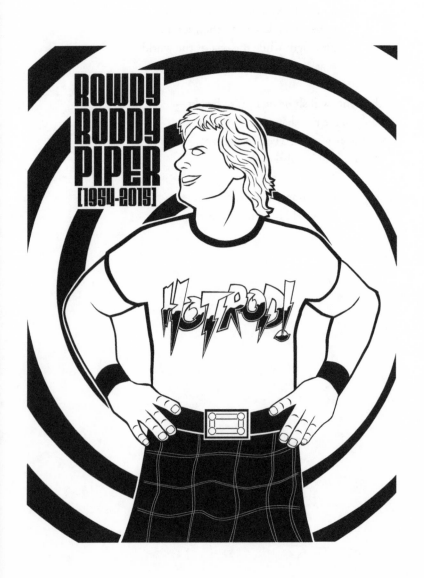

Adrian Adonis (1954-1988) died in a car accident.

Captain Lou Albano (1933-2009) died of a heart attack.

Andre the Giant (1946-1993) died in his sleep of heart failure.

Ox Baker (1934-2014) died of complications after a heart attack.

Penny Banner (1934-2008) died in her sleep.

Paul Bearer (1954-2013) died of natural causes.

Chris Benoit (1967-2007) hung himself after murdering his wife and son.

Woman, Nancy Benoit (1964-2007) was murdered by her husband.

The Big Boss Man (1963-2004) died of a heart attack.

Crusher Blackwell (1949-1995) died due to complications after a car accident.

Classy Freddie Blassie (1918-2003) died of heart and kidney failure.

Doink the Clown, Matt Borne (1957-2013) died of a drug overdose.

Bobo Brazil (1924-1998) died after a series of strokes.

Jack Brisco (1941-2010) died of complications after open heart surgery.

Bruiser Brody (1946-1988) was stabbed in a shower stall after a match in Puerto Rico.

Bad News Brown (1943-2007) died of a heart attack.

King Kong Bundy (1955-2019) died of complications from diabetes.

June Byers (1922-1988) died of pneumonia.

Chyna (1969-2016) died of a drug overdose.

Dick The Bruiser (1929-1991) died of internal bleeding after a ruptured blood vessel in his esophagus while lifting weights.

Earthquake (1963-2006) died after a long battle with cancer.

Miss Elizabeth (1960-2003) died of a drug and alcohol overdose.

Giant Baba (1938-1999) died of cancer.

Hot Stuff, Eddie Gilbert (1961-1995) died of a heart attack.

Terry Gordy (1961-2001) died of a heart attack.

Judy Grable (1935-2008) died in her home after suffering diabetes, multiple strokes and an early onset of Alzheimer's disease.

The Grand Wizard of Wrestling (1929-1983) died of a heart attack.

Eddie Guerrero (1967-2005) died of heart failure.

Owen Hart (1965-1999) died after falling from the stadium roof to the ring below.

Mr. Perfect Curt Hennig (1958-2003) died of a drug overdose.

Hercules Hernandez (1956-2004) died in his sleep as a result of heart disease.

The Super Destroyer, Don Jardine (1940-2006) died of complications resulting from a heart attack and leukemia.

Junkyard Dog (1952-1998) fell asleep while driving.

Gene Kiniski (1928-2010) died after a long battle with cancer.

'The Russian Bear' Ivan Koloff (1942-2017) died from liver cancer.

Killer Kowalski (1926-2008) died of a heart attack.

The Big Cat, Ernie Ladd (1938-2007) died after a long battle with colon cancer.

Strangler Ed Lewis (1891-1966) died in his sleep.

Crusher Lisowski (1926-2005) died of complications from a brain tumor.

Sherri Martel (1958-2007) died of a drug overdose.

Test, Andrew Martin (1975-2009) died of a drug overdose.

Wahoo McDaniel (1938-2002) died of complications due to renal failure and diabetes.

The Missing Link (1939-2007) died after a long battle with cancer.

Sputnik Monroe (1928-2006) died in his sleep.

Gorilla Monsoon (1937-1999) died of heart failure.

The Fabulous Moolah (1923-2007) died of either a heart attack or a blood clot.

Wayne Munn (1896-1931) died of acute inflammation of the kidneys.

Dick Murdoch (1946-1996) died of a heart attack.

Bronko Nagurski (1908-1990) died in a hospital bed.

Roddy Piper (1954-2015) died of a heart attack in his sleep.

Harley Race (1943-2019) died of lung cancer.

Road Warrior Animal (1960-2020) died of a heart attack.

Road Warrior Hawk (1957-2003) died of a heart attack.

Dusty Rhodes (1945-2015) died of kidney failure.

Rikidozan (1924-1963) died of peritonitis after being stabbed in his Tokyo night club.

The Nature Boy, Buddy Rogers (1921-1992) died after a series of strokes.

Playboy Buddy Rose (1952-2009) died in his home of natural causes.

Ravishing Rick Rude (1958-1999) died of heart failure and drug overdose.

Bruno Sammartino (1935-2018) died after multiple organ failure and heart problems.

The Macho Man, Randy Savage (1952-2011) died of a heart attack while driving.

Mad Dog, Buzz Sawyer (1959-1992) died of heart failure due to a drug overdose.

The Sheik (1924-2003) died of heart failure.

The British Bulldog, Davey Boy Smith (1962-2002) died of a heart attack.

Gordon Solie (1929-2000) died of throat cancer.

Stan Stasiak (1937-1997) died of heart failure.

Ray Stevens (1935-1996) died of a heart attack.

Chief Jay Strongbow (1928-2012) died of complications after falling at his home.

Big John Studd (1948-1995) died of liver cancer and Hodgkin's disease.

Lou Thesz (1916-2001) died after heart surgery.

Luna Vachon (1962-2010) died of a drug overdose.

Johnny Valentine (1928-2001) died in a hospital after falling off his porch.

David Von Erich (1958-1984) died of ruptured intestines from acute enteritis.

Kerry Von Erich (1960-1993) shot himself in the heart.

Gorgeous George Wagner (1915-1963) died of a heart attack.

Dr. Death, Steve Williams (1960-2009) died after a long battle with throat cancer.

Yokozuna (1966-2000) died of fluid in his lungs.

Mae Young (1923-2014) died of natural causes.

Yukon Eric (1924-1965) shot himself in a church parking lot.

Stanislaus Zbyszko (1879-1967) died of a heart attack.

"Chief Jay Strongbow Knows All About the Sleeper Hold" is after "Twenty-First Century" by Michael Collier.

"Polaroid of You and Jack Brisco" is after "1935" by Naomi Shihab Nye.

"Judy Grable Makes a Living" is after "The Question as Part of the Body" by Beckian Fritz Goldberg

ACKNOWLEDGMENTS

The Dead Wrestler Elegies was originally published in 2014 by Chicago press Curbside Splendor. When that publisher closed its doors in 2018, this book found itself out of print. The final section of this book is a continuation of the original edition, containing additional poems and illustrations, all new to this second edition.

Thank you to all the editors who have worked on the following anthologies and journals in which some of these poems have appeared previously, sometimes in different forms.

Boxcar Poetry Review: "Chief Jay Strongbow Knows All about the Sleeper Hold"

Cobalt Review: "Bronko Nagurski Beat Lou Thesz That Night," "It All Started with Strangler Lewis" and "Killer Kowalski and the Cauliflower Ear"

The Rupture (formerly *The Collagist*): "The Macho Man's Last Elbow Drop" and "Miss Elizabeth Said 'Oh Yeah'"

Copper Nickel: "Heart of the Texas Tornado" and "Selected Legends of Andre the Giant"

dislocate: "Gorilla Monsoon, Anything"

Eleven Eleven: "This is a Test," and "Where There's Blood There's Freddie Blassie"

From Parts Unknown: A Pro Wrestling Anthology: "Five Count for King Kong Bundy," "Harley Race and the Body Slam," and "Tonight, Bruno Sammartino and the Bearhug"

Heavy Feather Review: "The Grand Wizard of Wrestling Can Make You a Man," "Rikidozan was Big in Japan" and "The Missing Link Explains How to Be a Monster"

Menacing Hedge: "How I Know Stanislaus Zbyszko," "Judy Grable Makes a Living," and "June Byers Knows What a Woman Wants."

Moon City Review: "Ain't No Cage Can Hold Mad Dog Sawyer" and "Junkyard Dog Says Things Are Gonna Be All Right"

New Madrid: "Stan Stasiak Was World Champion for Nine Days"

New South: "David Von Erich Explains the Rules"

The Normal School: "Ask Terry Gordy Who He Is" and "Mae Young Has Always Been the Heel"

Paper Darts: "That Night the Fabulous Moolah Lost Her Championship," "Playboy Buddy Rose Knows how Much He Weighs," "Flowers for Adrian Adonis," "Hawk Leaves Animal Behind" and "Ravishing Rick Rude is Still the Sexiest Man"

The Pinch: "Ox Baker Explains the Heart Punch," "Remember Penny Banner," and "Where Bobo Brazil Lives"

Rabbit Ears: TV Poems: "Mr. Perfect Is What He Says He Is"

REAL: Regarding Arts & Letters: "Bruiser Brody Finishes This Thing," Every Night the Super Destroyer," "Gene Kiniski Says It's Not the End," "Sorrow for Woman," and "We Do Not Want to Believe There Is a Place in Hell."

Revolution House: "Behind Every Man Is Sensational Sherri," "New Hunting Grounds for Chief Wahoo McDaniel" and "The Sheik Likes to Hurt People"

RHINO: "Luna Vachon Is the Shadow in Your Darkness"

Tusculum Review: "Gorgeous George Was the Human Orchid"

Water~Stone Review: "Polaroid of You and Jack Brisco"

Waxwing: "A Box for Yokozuna," "A Man Is Not an Earthquake," "Paul Bearer Says We Are Not Alone," and "You Cannot Stand Before Giant Baba"

Willow Springs: "Be More Like Sputnik Monroe" and "Long
   Live the King of Hearts"
Winter Tangerine Review: "Eddie Guerrero's Last Frog Splash"

Thank you to Matthew Gavin Frank, Oliver de la Paz, Lee Ann
Roripaugh, Timothy Yu, Jacob Knabb, Patricia Clark, Austin
Bunn, Elena Passarello, Benjamin Drevlow, Sean Prentiss, Tony
Fulgham, Oindrila Mukherjee, Douglas S. Jones, Elizabyth
Hiscox, Jason Teal, and Alban Fischer. Thank you to Kundiman
faculty, staff and fellows. Thank you to my teachers at Arizona
State University. Thank you to all my colleagues and friends at
Grand Valley State University.

Thank you to Ander Monson and New Michigan Press for
printing this second edition. Thank you to the staff at Curbside
Splendor who supported the first edition of this book.

Thank you to my Poets Choice crew: Aaron Brossiet, Katie
Cappello, Ashley Cardona, Brian Clements, Brian Komei
Dempster, Judy Halebsky, Chris Haven, Amorak Huey, Amy
McInnis, Christina Olson, Dean Rader, Jean Prokott, and Mark
Schaub.

Thank you to the wrestlers and personalities of the pro
wrestling business, without whom these poems could not exist.

Thank you to my family, both immediate and extended. In
particular, thank you to my mother, father, and little sister.

And thank you to Caitlin Horrocks, my partner in life and
crime and everything in between, who continues to tie me in
knots after all these years.

W. TODD KANEKO is from Seattle, Washington. He is the author of the poetry books *This Is How the Bone Sings* and *The Dead Wrestler Elegies*, and co-author with Amorak Huey of *Slash / Slash* and *Poetry: A Writers' Guide and Anthology*. A Kundiman Fellow, he teaches at Grand Valley State University and lives with his family in Grand Rapids, Michigan.

❄

COLOPHON

Text is set in a digital version of Jenson, designed by Robert Slimbach in 1996, and based on the work of punchcutter, printer, and publisher Nicolas Jenson. The titles here are also in Jenson.

✳

NEW MICHIGAN PRESS, based in Tucson, Arizona, prints poetry and prose chapbooks, especially work that transcends traditional genre. Together with DIAGRAM, NMP sponsors a yearly chapbook competition.

DIAGRAM, a journal of text, art, and schematic, is published bimonthly at THEDIAGRAM.COM. Periodic print anthologies are available from the New Michigan Press at NEWMICHIGANPRESS.COM.